Interpretive Master Planning

FOR PARKS, HISTORIC SITES, FORESTS, ZOOS, AND RELATED TOURISM SITES.

FOR SELF-GUIDED INTERPRETIVE SERVICES

FOR INTERPRETIVE EXHIBITS

FOR GUIDED PROGRAMS/TOURS

John A. Veverka
April 1994

Exclusively Distributed by
The Interpretation, Publication, and Resource Center,
a Division of Pelham-Grayson, Inc.

Library of Congress Cataloging-in-Publication Data

Veverka, John A.
    Interpretive master planning : for parks, historic sites, forests, zoos, and
related tourism sites, for self-guided interpretive services, for interpretive exhibits,
for guided programs/tours/by John A. Veverka.
       p. cm.
    Includes bibliographical references.
    ISBN 1-56044-274-3
      1. Promotion of special events—Planning—Handbooks, manuals, etc.
2. Meetings—Planning—Handbooks, manuals, etc. 3. Recreation areas—
Interpretive programs—Planning—Handbooks, manuals, etc. 4. Historic
sites—Interpretive programs—Planning—Handbooks, manuals, etc.
5. Museum techniques—Handbooks, manuals, etc.
    I. Title.
    AS6.V48 1994   94-26220
    658.4'56—dc20   CIP

Printed in the United States of America.
Design, typesetting and other prepress work by Falcon Press, Helena, Montana.

Library of Congress Number 94-26220
ISBN # 1-56044-274-3

Foreword

Interpretors are as diverse as the resources they interpret. Whether they provide the experiences which enable visitors to enjoy and appreciate the magnificence of a calving glacier or the marine life along Alaska's Inside Passage or to understand the wrenching heartbreak of families divided by the Civil War, good interpretation comes from the heart and soul of the interpretor.

Interpretors actually are rather representative of the global melting pot. Through the years I have been impressed with the ability of interpretors to incorporate backgrounds as diverse as business management, psychology, political science and art into effective service in the field of interpretation. As professionals, our effectiveness is dependent upon the integration of knowledge gleaned from a myriad of sources and areas of expertise.

At some level of function, however, all interpretors will inevitably face the realization that great interpretation, while emanating from the heart, must also be based upon and incorporate the principles of good planning. Where are you? Where do you want to go? And how are you going to get there? Whether you are developing a program, an exhibit, a brochure, a trail, or a video project, understanding and being able to utilize a variety of types of planning processes will help you provide a more effective product.

I will never forget taking a group of my interpretive staff on a tour of a professional exhibit production facility several years ago. Upon noticing some scraps of velcro™ and foam core in one of the trash bins, one of them asked if it would be all right to take them. The approval unleashed a veritable scavenging party which was somewhat embarrassing, except that I was fully cognizant that to these folks the materials being thrown away truly represented a treasure of supplies they could and would use for exhibits in their various facilities. Most interpretors get used to scavenging, using whatever we can find, from whatever sources are available, because funds are usually restricted and supplies and resources limited. Thus, one of the basic skills of our profession has become "doing great things with nothing." We have learned out of necessity the ability to be efficient and effective.

Interpretors are committed to the search for a better way of meeting the needs of our visitors and agencies and to increasing public stewardship of our world tapestry of resources. This commitment is evidenced by the continual increase in participation in training opportunities, and to the eager reception of new interpretive materials. A common complaint heard is that so many of our professional colleagues are so involved in accomplishing great things that few have taken time out to put these great ideas on paper to be made available for others to incorporate into their operations and functions. Whenever one of our colleagues does produce a new tool, it is pounced on as eagerly as the velcro™ retrieved from the throw away barrel.

Well, *Interpretative Master Planning,* by John Veverka, is no recyled velcro™ folks! What this book does offer is an essential and fundamental tool for helping interpretors make the transition from idea to product as well as strategies for incorporating planning as a tool to increase the effectiveness of our processes and procedures.

John Veverka has provided a tool which should become a basic in every interpretive library.

Bobbie Gallup
Executive Director
National Association for Interpretation

Preface

A man's errors are his portals of discovery.
- James Joyce, Author

That quote may seem a strange way to start a preface, but it reflects the nature in which the content of this book came together. I started in interpretation "officially" in 1974 as a seasonal interpretor with Ohio State Parks. I had no formal training in interpretation—no real idea what it really was. My very first interpretive program was standing in front of 350 people in an amphitheater at Mohican State Park, in Ohio, for an evening slide program on "Snakes of the Park." As I gazed out on my first audience, with my heart pounding and sweat running down my neck, I can remember thinking, "Why am I doing this to myself?" My first program will not go down in history as anything but a "learning experience." Every mistake that could be made—I made it that night. And that was the real beginning of my education in interpretation.

While in the following years I did get my B.S. and Masters Degree in interpretation, and spent several years teaching interpretation in universities, in looking back I really never learned as much as I did from that experience that fateful night. What I learned was the truth of the above quotation. I learned I needed to try new things, to question the existing truths about interpretation, and to think about what interpretation can be instead of what it has been. In that pursuit I have made many errors (I prefer to call them either learning experiences or character-building experiences). But for every mistake I made I was rewarded with discovery as well.

This book is based on twenty years of learning experiences—of successes and the lessons learned from trying new ideas and strategies. We are always looking for new and better ways to do interpretation. The trick is to be willing to change when new ideas threaten old beliefs.

I focused this book on interpretive planning, mainly because none of the existing books really presented a good overview of how to do it. The philosophies and planning strategies presented here represent years of field testing—throwing out processes or ideas that sounded good in theory, but failed in the field, and building on processes and ideas that did work well in the field. My hope is that this book will serve as a good reference and field tool for you on how to do interpretive planning. But while I have found these ideas work well for me, and use them in my daily business, I would hope that you will look for new and better ways to do interpretation and planning. Try to improve or expand on the ideas presented here. Don't be afraid to challenge, question, and explore new ways of doing things. Never be satisfied with the way things are, or are being done. You can always do better. That's how our profession will grow and evolve—by doing new things and by the discoveries made from the doing.

John A. Veverka
Dansville, Michigan

Acknowledgments

In putting together a book like this one, which reflects twenty or more years of learning, discussions, attending conferences, reading journals, and so on, it is impossible to name all of the people who have contributed to the ideas presented here. Thanks to all of the interpretors who were willing to share ideas at national conferences and through journal articles.

There are two individuals I would like to thank for their years of friendship and professional association, Alan Capelle and Gary Moore. They have been a sounding board for most of my crazy ideas, provided outstanding assistance on numerous projects, and have been a source of support and inspiration.

In addition, I would like to thank the folks who took their time to serve as reviewers for this book: Bobbie Gallup, Executive Director, National Association for Interpretation; Richard Hoffman, Region 8 Interpretive Specialist for the USDA Forest Service; Roy Underhill, Director of Interpretive Development for the Colonial Williamsburg Foundation; Gary Mullins, Interpretation Program at The Ohio State University; Bill Lewis, Communication Professor, University of Vermont; and Alan Capelle, State Historical Society of Wisconsin.

I would like to give a special note of appreciation to Dr. Gabe Cherem. Gabe was my Interpretation Professor when I attended Ohio State University in the 1970s and my first mentor. He taught me the foundations of interpretation philosophy, theory, and techniques I still use today.

I would also like to give a special thanks to Dr. Bill Lewis, my second mentor. I first met Bill several years ago when fate brought us together to teach a U.S. Army Corps of Engineers training program. That first training course, and the many that Bill and I have taught together since then, was another great learning experience for me. Bill is indeed a "master interpretor." His gentle, powerful, and skillful presentations, and his deep concern for and communication with the audience, always impresses me. I have learned an enormous amount by just sitting back and watching him in action.

Finally, I would like to thank my wife Judi, and children Joseli, Jovetta, and Jynell, for their support and understanding. They still don't quite understand what an "interpretor" is, or what it is I do when I go to work, yet they put up with me anyway. But I have had to promise them when we go to zoos, museums, nature centers, or any place else that has interpretation on our family vacations that I will keep quiet and not take so many photographs of exhibits, interpretive signs, and so on. I'm sure that you interpretors out there know what I'm talking about.

Table of Contents

List of Photographs

List of Tables

List of Figures

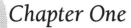

Chapter One

Interpreting to Visitors—
Learning Concepts

*Creative thinking may simply mean the realization
that there's no particular virtue in doing things the way
they have always been done.*

- Rudolph Flesch, Educator

Why Are We Here—
Remember the Visitor?

Before we plunge into the many aspects of interpretive philosophy, theory, and planning, it's important to ask WHY ARE WE HERE? What is the main objective of interpretive programs and services?

Simply stated, our primary mission as interpretors is to communicate with our visitors.

I have found that most interpretors* boast high levels of knowledge about certain resources or special fields (geology, natural history, cultural history, etc.). And many have a fairly good foundation in communication principles. But I have also found that many interpretors know too little about understanding visitors. It seems that many academic courses for interpretors leave out key areas of study, such as visitor psychology. Students of interpretation learn how to present programs and services, but are left in the dark when it comes to how or why visitors learn and remember information.

Throughout this text, the spelling interpretor is used to distinguish the profession from that of an interpreter (or translator) of foreign languages.

To remedy this situation, interpretors and students in training should consider broadening their education to include (at a minimum) the following important subjects:

- Adult non-formal education (adults as learners).
- Consumer Behavior
- Marketing and advertising courses
- The psychology of the audience (theater or psychology department)

It's not enough to work hard to make our programs interesting and exciting. We must also understand what motivates visitors to participate and how best to apply our communication skills and procedures used in adult education. We must study how to use marketing strategies to grab the visitors' attention and feed their desire to remember the interpretive message, to carry it home with them. If we fail, the visitor may choose to not participate, or may quickly forget all that was "learned."

Understanding the psychology of the visitor in recreational settings is essential to developing successful interpretive plans. Let's take a little time here at the beginning to look at some of the general concepts I have found to be the most valuable when planning and designing interpretive programs and services.

Recreational Learning

I use the term *recreational learning* to describe the kind of learning that visitors to parks, forests, historic sites, zoos, and so on are usually most interested in. It is important to recognize that, in many cases, the main reason people are visiting a site is not for a purely interpretive experience. For example, the main activities of interest cited by most zoo visitors are picnicking and being with friends and family. Seeing the animals is often third. Learning about the animals is way down the list.

In a park or forest, the main reason for visitors coming to the site is for the array of recreational activities available (camping, hiking, fishing, boating, etc.). Taking part in interpretive programs or activities is NOT a main reason for the visit. Remember that the visitor is in a "vacation frame of mind" and wants to have fun (to recreate). Thus, any learning activity should also be a recreational activity. Interpretive services must promote the notion that learning is fun and enjoyable. In this light, learning about the environment, animals, history, or any other topic becomes, for the visitor, another recreational opportunity.

A recreational learning experience should also encourage the visitor to "self select" those learning opportunities that he or she finds interesting or fun. This places a heavy burden on our abilities to advertise interpretive programs in ways that *provoke* visitor interest and to *relate* the interpretive message to their every-day lives, giving visitors a reason to select our program or service over some other recreational activity. (Knowing how to *provoke* and *relate* to visitors is important; these skills are explained further in Chapter Two.)

If you are not sure yet what "recreational learning" is, the best example is any hobby that you might have. Whether you are a bird watcher, coin collector, or Civil War buff, you probably enjoy reading and learning more about your particular field of interest. The hobby itself is a recreational activity. The time you spend reading books or magazines about your hobby to increase your expertise in it is recreational learning.

As an interpretive planner, you MUST be aware that this is the frame of mind that most of your visitors are probably in. They don't want to become experts in the subject you are presenting, they just want to have fun learning about the site or topic at hand. Remember what Freeman Tilden (1957) said about interpretation: "The chief aim of interpretation is provocation, not instruction."

How Can We Get Visitors to Learn and Remember Information in a Recreational Learning Environment?

OK, so just what is involved in helping visitors to remember the information that we are presenting to them? Here are some learning concepts and principles, along with four activities that will give you a better understanding of how people learn and remember. These activities were developed by Dr. Bill Lewis for interpretor training courses. I have used them in my training for several years now...and they work.

Learning Concepts:

There are several important learning concepts for interpretors to understand. These include:

- We all bring our pasts to the present.
- Categories can blind us.
- First impressions are especially important.
- Unless helped, we often fail to find, see, or comprehend.
- To understand the parts, we must first see the whole.
- Discovery makes learning fun.
- Meanings are in people, not words.
- Information overload causes distortion and fatigue.
- Simplicity and organization clarify messages.
- A picture can be worth a thousand words.

Here are four activities I use (you can use them too) to help people understand these and other learning concepts.

Activity 1

This activity has a lot of impact in my training courses. I have participants listen to a classical music tape and ask them to write down on a piece of paper what the music makes them think of. After about three to four minutes of listening to the tape, I go around the room and see what their responses to the music are. Some common responses I have garnered from this exercise include:

- Masterpiece theater
- A Royal Procession
- A Walt Disney Movie
- Butterflies floating in the wind
- An old English movie.
- Going to the symphony
- Hated the music
- Don't like classical stuff

...and the list goes on.

Then we discuss what similarities the group can find in the responses (what similarities do you see?). We also discuss the ability of music to create a mental picture or to provoke memories in people of past places, events, etc.

After discussion of this exercise, I next play a tape of the Beatles "I Want To Hold Your Hand" for the group, and repeat the exercise. Again, we discuss similarities from the responses. Of course, many of the participants relate to this music differently than they did to the classical music. Many can recall the 1960s, and relate on a personal basis ("I remember...") to what was going on at the time, such as the Vietnam War, the Ed Sullivan Show, and other events.

After this discussion, I then tell them that the great disparity in their responses has caused a slight problem. The first "classical" music they heard and the Beatles music just played are, in fact, the same song. I replay the first recording and point out the now obvious "I Want To Hold Your Hand" rhythm (now accompanied by groans from the participants). This first tape is from a classical version of Beatles songs called "The Beatles Go Baroque." So why didn't they hear the Beatles tune the first time around?

Most say that it only took a few seconds for them to "classify" the music as Classical, and the images that the music stimulated took only seconds to form in their mind.

The Learning Concepts illustrated by this exercise include:

- First impressions are especially important.
- Categories can blind us.

You can do this exercise in your own training if you want. There are several different tapes of Beatles music done in "classical" formats that will work just as well.

Activity 2

In this learning activity I show the group a slide on a screen. The catch is—they can't look at the slide (I ask them to cover their eyes; no peeking). Then I ask one participant to describe the slide to the group.

After the person tries his or her best to describe the slide, I then allow the group to look at the slide to see if their "mental picture" was close to the one actually on the screen. In the vast majority of cases it isn't even close. Some thought the image would be closer, some imagined a different perspective, some added stuff to the picture and some left stuff out, and all sorts of other differences emerge.

A realization grows on the group that people tend to inject images from past experiences into their mental photo. For example, if the describer said it was a picture of a lake, most participants conjured up a picture in their mind of a lake with which *they* were familiar. If the describer said "a tall tree," the participants visualized the "tallest tree" they had in their mental image reference libraries.

The Learning Concepts illustrated by this exercise include:

- We all brings our pasts to the present.
- Meaning are in people, not words. We all carry our own mental "image dictionaries" of words. Any given word means different things to different people. My big lake and your big lake will have different mental visual examples (*my* big lake is not *your* big lake).
- A picture can be worth a thousand words.

Another concept that the exercise illustrates has a design function as well. If you use photos in your brochures or exhibits, and have little or no captions for the photos, what is the visitor actually seeing? Do you have "recreation" photos with no visitors or people in them? What message does that send to people looking at the brochure. Remember: A lot of visitors can look at the same photo and "see" different things.

Always make sure that your photos or graphics do accurately illustrate their intended purpose. If you're not sure, test them on a group (of friends or colleagues) to see what their perceptions of the photo or graphic are.

Here is one of the photos I use in my training exercise. How would you describe this? On a piece of paper write down your description of the photo. Look on the last page of this chapter to find out what this photo actually depicts.

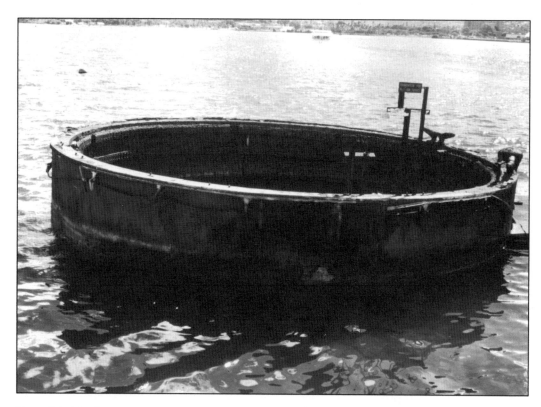

Describe this photo.

Chapter One Interpreting to Visitors—Learning Concepts

Activity 3

WHAT IS IT? Take a look at this graphic. I'm not going to tell you what it is, or even if this is the right way to look at it (it may be upside down!). But it is a graphic of something that you have seen before.

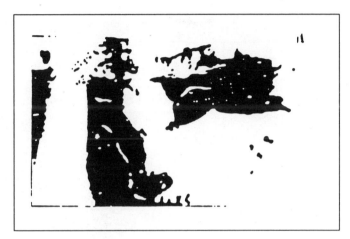

Figure 1. What is it?

If you can't figure it out, look at Figure 3 on page 9 (the cow). This first graphic (Figure 1) is a close up of part of the cow shown in the second graphic, a close up of the cow's head. Using the complete picture of the cow, see if you can now find the cow's head in the above graphic.

The Learning Concepts illustrated by this exercise include:

- To understand the parts, we must first see the whole.
- Unless helped, we often fail to find, see, or comprehend.

Remember that visitors really need to understand the whole (the big picture, the *theme*) before they can more easily find and understand the parts of the whole. Why do you think this is important for an interpretive planner to know?

Also bear in mind that it is the role of the interpretor to help visitors "see" and comprehend the story being interpreted. Be sure they understand the whole picture before giving lots of details on separate elements of the story.

Activity 4

Take a look at the six word boxes below (Figure 2). Can you find the words hidden in each of them? The answer to box 1 is "sand box." See if you can figure out the answers to the other ones. The answers are on the last page of this chapter.

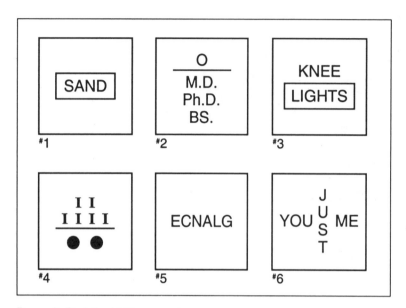

Figure 2. Find the hidden meaning.

Notice how you feel when you discover the answer. Did you get a sense of a door opening and "seeing" what you didn't see before? That brief sense of joy of having solved the puzzle, that spark of excitement or accomplishment, of *understanding*, is the big payoff. This is the reward that each visitor should feel during interpretive programs, whether conducted by an interpretor or self-guided, when the answer or information is "revealed" to them.

If someone gave you a hint to help solve one of the puzzles, how did that affect your sense of discovery?

The Learning Concepts illustrated by this exercise include:

- Unless helped, we often fail to find, see, or comprehend.
- Discovery makes learning fun.

Back to the Cow?

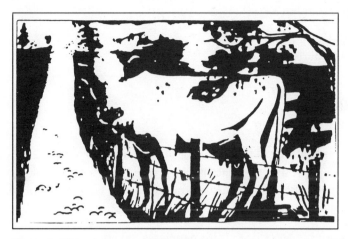

Figure 3. This picture should help you discover the identity of the graphic in Activity 3.

Learning Concept Summary

Go back to page 3 and review the list of learning concepts. Can you think of any activities to illustrate how categories can blind us or how information overload causes distortion and fatigue? You may want to discuss each concept and think of more examples of each as well. How could you use these in past programs? How can you use these in any future program or activity planning?

Learning Principles Summary

In addition to the learning concepts, here are some learning principles (also from Bill Lewis) that most of the activities help bring out. As an interpretive planner, be aware of these principles as you plan interpretive programs and services.

- People learn better when they're actively involved in the learning process.
- People learn better when they're using as many senses as appropriate.
- People prefer to learn that which is of most value to them at the present.
- That which people discover for themselves generates a special and vital excitement and satisfaction.
- Learning requires activity on the part of the learner.
- Friendly competition stimulates learning.
- Knowing the usefulness of the knowledge being acquired makes learning more effective.
- People learn best from hands-on experiences.
- Questions can be effectively used to help people derive meanings.
- Giving people expectations at the beginning of an activity will focus attention and thus improve learning.
- The ways in which people are responded to affects their learning.

What do Visitors Remember?

Besides these learning concepts and principles, here is some other information about visitor memory retention in general (Lewis 1988).

Visitors remember about:

10 percent of what they hear
30 percent of what they read
50 percent of what they see
90 percent of what they do

Now, what are the implications of this information? As an interpretor planning a variety of services and media for your site or facility, how effective do you think an interpretive talk without visual aids would be? If visitors remember only ten percent of what you said, was your talk a success?

Suppose you're developing wayside exhibit panels. What should go on the panel? If you rely mostly on text, you will be "mostly" ineffective in having visitors actually remember anything (thirty percent) for the long term. If you add appropriate graphics (remembering what we learned from the learning concepts and principles earlier), you might increase information retention to fifty percent. But look what happens when activities are suggested on the exhibit panel, such as:

- Look for the....
- See if you can find....
- Can you hear (or smell) the...?
- Go ahead and touch the.....

By planning and designing-in behaviors to encourage interaction (doing) with each panel, you may be able to increase information retention to ninety percent!

As a rule of thumb, when I plan or design interpretive exhibit panels for wayside exhibits or self-guiding trail stops, I strive for a design (if it's appropriate for that location and the story) that:

- Is highly visual (a picture is worth a thousand words).
- Encourages interaction (people remember ninety percent of what they do).
- Keeps text short and interpretive (see Chapter Four).

These ideas, and other design considerations, are discussed in greater detail in chapters Four and Five.

Some Interesting and Useful Ideas About Visitor Psychology

Perceptions - A Pig Story

There was a man who really loved to drive his sports car as quickly up a winding road as he could. He could hardly wait to get off from work just so he could do this winding drive. One day he was zipping along up the winding road when a woman in a car came skidding around a blind corner, swerving into his lane as she made the turn, and almost running the man and his car off the road. As she swept by him she leaned her head out her window and screamed at him "PIG!" He, in turn, screamed back at her "SOW!" He continued making his turn around the bend and drove head on into...a pig that was standing in the road.

We have learned in this chapter that one person's perception of the world may not be the same as someone else's. It is also important to remember that visitors' perceptions of the world, the agency you might work for, the concept of stewardship, or any other topic or event, are never wrong. They are just *different*. In a room full of people, some of the folks will think the room is cold, some will think that it is hot, and others will think the temperature is just right. And all of them are right.

The other thing we have to remember as interpretive planners is that we cannot change the visitors' perceptions. Only THE VISITORS can change their perceptions. Our job is to communicate evidence, to gently use persuasion strategies, and to create opportunities for them to make a discovery or to change their views—their perceptions—on their own. Our job is to employ a strategy for change.

So how do we develop such a strategy? This is something that advertising and marketing firms have been doing for a long time.

First, we must learn how to effectively harness the concept of *cognitive dissonance*. What this means is that we must find a way to take the foundation of existing beliefs that a visitor may have about an issue or agency, and create uncertainty or *dissonance* in his or her mind about the validity of these beliefs. This strategy is used in almost every advertisement that runs on television or in magazines to get consumers to try new products. Here are a few examples.

EXAMPLE 1

Belief a person may have: "Absolve" is the best laundry detergent.

Goal of advertising firm: Convince people that Absolve is NOT the best laundry detergent—new and improved "Dazzle" is the best laundry detergent.

Create dissonance in existing belief: Show dirty laundry being washed using both detergents; the pile of clothes washed with Dazzle "looks" whiter!

Supporting evidence: Testimonials from "average person" to validate the idea that Dazzle is better.

Emotional objective: Make viewers feel guilty (not a good parent, etc.) if they don't want the cleanest possible clothes for their family.

Desired behavioral change: Try new Dazzle instead of Absolve (or viewers' other normal brands).

EXAMPLE 2

Belief a person may have: Resource conservation is not something I need to worry about or be actively involved in.

Goal of agency: Convince visitors that they all need to take some pro-active role in conservation and that it can benefit them directly.

Create dissonance in existing belief: Show visitors that their involvement is necessary for the conservation of a particular resource, and how using some simple conservation activities at home can benefit them and the environment.

Supporting evidence: Use a variety of photographs, testimonials, group pressure from clubs or organizations, demonstrations, etc. to provide visual support of benefits.

Emotional objective: Make visitors feel a little "guilty" about not using good conservation at home. Or when visiting other sites, make them feel that implementing conservation activities at home is "really easy to do," doesn't cost a lot, and will make them feel good when they do it. (Remove the *risk* from trying it).

Desired behavioral change: To encourage visitors to take a pro-active approach to resource conservation, both on-site and at home. To get visitors to try one or two simple resource conservation activities at home, and eventually, to promote more involvement or support of conservation.

A Quick Exercise

For a fun exercise, take a look at TV commercials, ads in magazines, or even look at some of your own existing publications or educational materials. Are they (are you) using dissonance strategies to promote behavioral or perceptual changes in people? If you aren't, could you? How?

Figure 4 illustrates in a more visual way how a perception and behavioral change strategy might be structured, based on interpretive objectives discussed in more detail in Chapter Three.

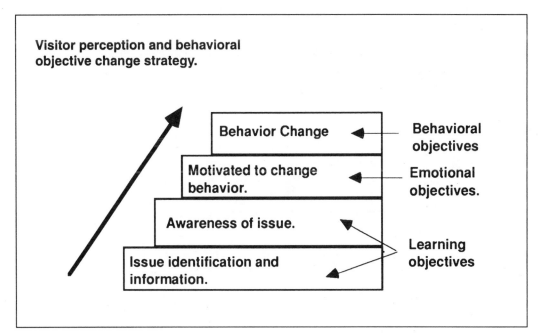

Figure 4.

This illustration shows the four basic steps of any simple change strategy. First, we present information to visitors about the issue. Then we create and enhance visitor awareness of the issue. This is followed by providing the visitors with motivation to change, and then with any luck, the change occurs. Some change strategies may be accomplished by a single program, while other more complex issues may take months or years for the desired behavior to occur in large numbers of people.

Visitors and Their Motives or Needs

Human motives or needs are an important area of study, based largely on A. H. Maslow's (1954) hierarchy of needs. Understanding visitors' needs can directly affect our interpretive planning strategies for programs and services (Figure 5).

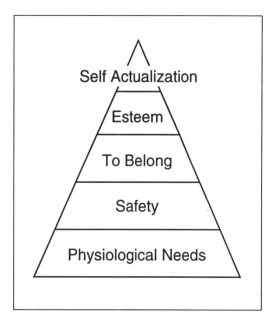

Figure 5. Maslow's Hierarchy of Needs.

This hierarchy of needs begins with physiological needs, and moves up to self-actualization needs. Let's take a closer look at these needs visitors have, and how they can influence our interpretive planning considerations.

Physiological Needs

Physiological needs are our first and most primal or basic needs. If we are too hot, too cold, uncomfortable, thirsty, hungry, or have to use the bathroom, our particular need takes overriding control of us. This is crucial, for example, in planning a visitor center: the most important consideration for visitors is ease in finding and using the bathrooms and drinking fountains. In planning an interpretive trail, think about where visitors might become hot or tired (where to put benches or shade?). I have planned one interpretive trail where, because of physiological considerations, I knew that the trail would not be used in summer. From June through first frost, this trail is very hot, very humid, and thick with bugs. Most visitors would not enjoy the trail at all given these factors. I have also seen some trails that visitors entered only to turn back within a few minutes, mosquitoes driving them out. If visitors spend too much time on a guided trail smacking bugs, itching, and scratching, then what's probably foremost on their minds is getting back to the car, not a desire to learn about wildflowers.

When leading guided programs think about your visitors' physiological needs. Is the sun in their eyes while you're talking to them? Are they hot and tired? Once visitors become uncomfortable, they stop paying attention to learning and listening, and the need for relief takes over. You cannot interpret to hot and tired visitors and expect their full attention.

A planner must always consider the visitor's physiological needs in all aspects of site, facility, and program or services planning.

Safety Needs

Next in the hierarchy of needs are the safety needs. If visitors perceive the event or activity as being "dangerous," or if they are "at risk" in any way, they will think twice about participating in the activity.

I select my day trips, camping sites, etc., by asking myself, "Would this be a safe place for me or my family to visit?"

Visitor orientation is also part of the safety motive. Visitors often suffer "trip stress" when trying to find an unfamiliar recreation site.

Remember this when planning and providing interpretive facilities and services. Build in reassurances for all visitors that your site will be easy to find and offers a safe environment for them to recreate. Also realize, however, that some risks—such as mountain climbing or whitewater rafting—are desired by select visitors.

In interpretation, visitors' concern for safety can be used to market programs. For example, when I was a seasonal interpretor with Ohio State Parks we advertised our "snake program" by noting in our schedule that "There are two kinds of poisonous snakes found in this park. What should you or your children do if you encounter a snake here in the park? Come to our Wednesday night program *How to survive living in a campground—a snake's point of view!* to find out what to do if you see a snake." This appeal to the safety motive got us a packed amphitheater for our evening program.

The Need to Belong

For the most part, people are gregarious, preferring companionship to solitude. It's rare to find anyone visiting a park, historic site, museum, or forest alone. Families, in particular, seek out activities that they can do as a family, or with a larger group. In addition, groups provide safety (there's safety in numbers, or at least people who can help you if you need it).

Esteem Needs

People like to build on their feelings of self worth, and learning (in any format) contributes to that self esteem. In interpretation, this is a major motive for visitors attending interpretive programs and services. We all share the desire to improve ourselves, and doing so is generally regarded as fun, as recreational learning. Remember that people learn most effectively when they are praised for trying, when they feel comfortable and safe, and when their accomplishments are recognized.

The Need for Self Actualization

Maslow says that we never fully self-actualize, but are always working toward that end. What is self actualization?

Perhaps the best definition is the Army slogan, to "be all you can be." At various times in our lives, each of us wants to be smarter, more physically fit, more creative, more skilled—in short, closer to fulfilling our potential. Learning through interpretation can help meet this need by encouraging people to explore new ideas and become more well-rounded.

These are the basic motives that we all harbor, the needs that drive us to pursue a variety of activities (not just interpretive ones). In Chapter Three we will take a closer look at studies in which researchers tried to determine which motives drove park visitors to select and attend interpretive programs and services, based on Maslow's hierarchy.

References

Atkinson, J. W. 1964. *An Introduction to Motivation.* D. Van Nostrand Co. Inc. NY.

Lewis, William J. 1988. *Interpreting for Park Visitors.* Eastern National Park & Monument Association, Philadelphia, PA.

Maslow, A. H. 1954. *Motivations and Personality.* Harper & Row Publishers, NY.

Tilden, Freeman. 1967. *Interpreting Our Heritage.* The University of North Carolina Press.

Veverka, J. A. 1978. *A Survey and Analysis of Selected Park Visitors' Motivations for Attending Environmental Interpretation Programs.* M.S. Thesis, Ohio State University.

Answers to Activities:

The Mystery Photograph

The photo on page 6 is of a gun turret on the USS Arizona, taken from the USS Arizona Memorial in Pearl Harbor, Hawaii.

Word box solutions (Figure 2):

1 - Sand box
2 - Three degrees below zero
3 - Neon lights
4 - Dark circles under the eyes
5 - A backwards glance
6 - Just between you and me

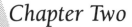

Chapter Two

Introduction to Interpretation

I don't like to eat snails. I prefer fast food.
- Strange de Jim, Pundit

Before we can begin to discuss how to do interpretive services master planning, site planning, or project planning for a park, forest, historic site, or other site, or individual interpretive services planning, such as for a self-guided trail or tour, we must first understand precisely what *interpretation* is. This word has had almost as many meanings as there are people using it. Yet one definition of interpretation suits our purposes better than all others. It was developed by Interpretation Canada in 1976 and articulates the basic concepts of interpretation:

> *Interpretation is a communication process designed to reveal meanings and relationships of our cultural and natural heritage to the public (visitors) through first-hand experiences with objects, artifacts, landscapes, or sites.*

The most important item to remember here is that interpretation is not a thing, but rather a very specific type of communication **process**.

What is the Process of Interpretation?

Any form of communication that we may have with visitors usually involves two basic communication styles. We present the materials we want the visitor to know in an *informational* style, or in an *interpretive* style. The difference between the two styles is not *what* we present but *how* we present it. Informational styles simply dispense the facts, the way a field guide lists and describes species, for example. But the interpretive style reveals a story or larger message, relying on Tilden's Principles (see below) to help the visitor relate to that message.

When communicating with visitors using the interpretive approach, the main goal of the interpretor is to translate from the technical language of experts to the "everyday" language of the visitor. This is known as *conceptual translation*.

The interpretive communication process is based on Tilden's six Interpretive Principles, which state:

1. Any interpretation that does not somehow **relate** what is being displayed or described to something within the personality or experience of the visitor will be sterile.
   - Talk to your visitors before the program and relate your program to them using the information you've gained about them.
   - Ask yourself, "Why would my visitors want to know the information I am giving them?"
   - People of different age groups or from different regions of the country often have different interests, motives, or expectations of your program or services. Do you know what these are, and how to best relate your messages to visitors' diverse needs?

2. Information, as such, is not interpretation. Interpretation is **revelation** based upon information. These are entirely different things. All interpretation, however, includes information.

3. Interpretation is **an art**, which combines many arts, whether the materials presented are scientific, historical, or architectural. Any art is in some degree teachable.
   - In one evening program you may be a teacher, actor, or story teller.

4. The chief aim of interpretation is not instruction, but **provocation**.
   - Your role is to help change attitudes and behavior, to motivate, to inspire, to take information and make it meaningful, interesting, and exciting.
   - Your ultimate objective is to take the visitor through the process of sensitivity-awareness-understanding-appreciation and finally, commitment.

5. Interpretation should aim to **present a whole rather than a part**, and must address itself to the whole person rather than any phase.
   - In all programs, exhibits, or other media, you will achieve better results if you concentrate on only one theme for the entire program or service, and come up with various ways to express or illustrate that theme.
   - Help visitors understand that the things they do and see in the park or site are related to what they do and see at home in their everyday lives.

6. Interpretation addressed to **children** (say, up to the age of twelve) should not be a dilution of the presentation to adults, but should **follow a fundamentally different approach**. To be at its best it will require a separate program.

I use a short-hand version of these principles to reinforce the main communication procedures. I call these *Tilden's Tips*. The main points for the Tips, and the process that I feel makes a communication "interpretive" rather than just informational, are:

Provoke - Begin the interpretation with a provocative statement, title, or other technique to get the visitors' attention and stimulate interest in the communication to follow. In an exhibit, for example, a provocative title might be "Sex on the Rocks!", interpreting the procreation of coastal marine life that lives on rocks. Unless you can grab and hold on to the visitors' attention and interest, you will not succeed in communicating with them.

Relate - Tilden states that unless we can help the visitor relate the essence or importance of our message or story to the everyday lives of the visitors, the message will be sterile. Thus, we need to use a variety of techniques (analogies, metaphors, etc.) to help the visitor identify with the message.

As an example, I was observing a program at a historical site and the docent was interpreting to a group of fifth graders how pioneer women used flat irons to iron their clothes. Most of the group seemed disinterested in this presentation (do fifth graders really care about ironing?). Then one young man raised his hand and asked, "Why did they have to iron?" He didn't understand why people ironed clothes back then, but don't do it now. You see, he had never seen anyone in his home use an iron—all of their clothes are "perma-press." So this program did not connect with the fifth graders on a lot of different levels.

Reveal - Revelation is the "best part of the story or presentation." It gives visitors the answer, through a unique or unusual viewpoint.

Address The Whole - This tip refers to the importance of having one unifying theme for your program, exhibits, master plan, etc. The importance of the theme and how to develop one will be discussed later in this book.

Strive for Message Unity - Use a sufficient but varied repetition of cues to create and support a particular theme, mood, or aura.

I was attending a guided hike one day when I observed a typical situation where an interpretor missed the boat by "not interpreting" to a young man on the trail who had asked a question. The boy, pointing to an ash tree, asked the interpretor what kind of tree it was. The interpretor looked at the tree, then at the boy, and said, "It's an ash tree." At that point, the communication stopped—and so did any meaningful interpretive learning experience. By using Tilden's Tips the interpretor could have said something like:

"Have you ever seen a baseball game on TV? Do you remember how everyone gets all excited when the batter hits a home run? Well, without this tree, or ones like it, that home run may not have happened. You see—this

is the baseball bat tree! *Most baseball bats are made out of the wood from ash trees just like this one. So the next time you see a baseball game, think about this old ash tree, and your hike with us today!"*

Can you identify how the Tips were used in the above interpretation?

Here is another short example of interpretive writing illustrating how Tilden's Tips can be used.

"At first glance this small bone might not look like much, but if we take a closer look at it we will see that this is the jaw bone of one of the most vicious and ferocious animals ever to live in the forest *(provoke). It is a* relentless hunter *(provoke), spending all of its time in search of any victims he is able to overcome and eat. In fact, in order to stay alive, this animal must eat* several times its own body weight every day *(provoke) just to stay alive. Just imagine, if this creature were the size of a large dog, it would need to eat about 500 pounds of meat a day (relate). Now 500 pounds is a lot! That's about 3 1/2 park visitors a day (relate and reveal)!*

Well, luckily for us, this animal is only a few inches long *(provoke) when full grown. This is the* jaw of a shrew *(reveal), an animal that looks like a small mouse (relate), but has the* heart of a tiger *(relate). Now if you look closely at the jaw as I pass it around* can you see anything unusual about its teeth *(provoke)? They're colored red and black at the base of each tooth. The* shrews are the only group of animals that have red and black teeth *(reveal), and that's the secret to identifying this animal.*

Now, do any of you clip coupons for grocery shopping *(provoke and relate)? Well, get your coupon clippers ready. Just up ahead we're going to see* where the shrews go food shopping *(relate and provoke). So let's go up the trail a bit and see what's for dinner today."*

Verbal and Non-verbal Communication

As we present any form of interpretive program or service, we are using both verbal and non-verbal communication techniques. Each of these techniques has elements that help us to develop the content and structure of the interpretive message.

Verbal Communication

To understand the role of verbal communication in interpretation, the main point to consider is that the words we use—or how we say them—may convey many hidden messages as well.

Examples of how we might use active language to perk up a talk or text include:

Active verbs - leaves *crunch* and *crumble* beneath your feet.
Personal words - You, yours, we, she, they.
Theme words - Husband, female, suitor, bride
Colorful nouns - thief, enthusiasm
Powerful adjectives - *booted* feet, *blood-red* leaves.

Remember, the words we select to use in interpretive messages are important to consider. You may recall from Chapter One that meanings are in people, not in words. We each may have our own visual dictionary or vocabulary of reference for any given word. Thus, the word "lake" may have many different interpretations for different visitors, depending on the lakes that they may have seen or be experienced with. When someone says the word "lake," we often use our own "lake" visual reference to give us a mental image of what the person is talking about.

Painting with words is a tool utilized by many interpretors, authors, and storytellers. They select words that stimulate a mental image for the visitor—using the words as a mental paintbrush so the visitor can visualize the scene or activity. For example, instead of saying to visitors "imagine an autumn evening" and leaving it at that, you might say "imagine walking in the woods on a clear cold night, the white frozen mist of your breath gleaming in the moonlight as dried leaves crunch and crumble beneath your feet!"

Remember, words have hidden meanings for each visitor...choose them carefully.

Words to Avoid!

There are many words that we see in publications, signs, and exhibits or hear in live presentations that are best avoided. These are words with *no visual reference* for the visitor. For example, you may tell the visitor that a particular site is five acres in size. Consider that most visitors have never "seen" an acre! Most have no visual reference for just how big an acre is. If you don't give them an analogy or some visual frame of reference (the land that X number of homes in your neighborhood may take up), this is useless information for the visitor. There are lots of other words like this, including technical terms for which visitors may not have any frame of reference. These include:

> Cubic acres of water in the lake.
> Cubic feet of water per second going over the spillway.
> Board feet of timber.
> A cord of wood.
> Deciduous forest.
> Coniferous forest.
> 500 pounds (or any weight greater than 150 pounds or so).
> Miles.
> Any others you can add to this list?

I was leading a guided hike years ago with a school group, and one of the students told me that he was afraid to go into the woods because he thought that coniferous forests ate meat! Don't use words that may confuse visitors unless you give the visitor a good visual definition of what that word means.

Always ask yourself, "Will visitors know what I'm talking about? Do they understand the vocabulary I am using?"

For some interpretive services (such as self-guiding cassette tapes for trails or auto tours), the verbal message is everything. Background music, the type of voice (male or female, old or young, kind of accent), are all part of creating the desired image. They are also key components of relating to your audience and presenting a unified message.

Non-verbal Communication

In general, we are a visually oriented people. We "read" the landscape, people, situations, and day-to-day activities with our eyes. We deduce meanings from what we see in non-verbal cues all around us, from international traffic signs, people's posture, or the red glow of a stove's heating element. We are always scanning and reading. Other senses—hearing, taste, touch, and smell—also come into play. Some of the elements of non-verbal communication include:

Sounds	Texture	Use of space
Odor	Colors	Body language
Taste	Symbols	Time

It is important to remember that most of our interpretive services involve interpreting concepts and meanings of the world around us through these non-verbal cues. Every publication and brochure, wayside exhibit, or visitor center exhibit communicates mainly through non-verbal cues. These will be discussed in more detail in the following chapters.

When designing interpretive programs or services bear in mind that visitors retain:

10 percent of what they hear.
30 percent of what they read.
50 percent of what they see.
90 percent of what they do.

Where Did These Principles Come From? Why do They Work?

In case this basic communication strategy looks familiar (and it should), this is a strategy used in journalism and just about all marketing or advertising programs today. Think of any good commercial or magazine ad you have seen. The ad first has to get your attention. If it doesn't, a potential sale will be lost. So all good ads **provoke** attention, curiosity, or interest. Secondly, each ad strives to **relate** to each target market why the consumer needs the product. The ads also **reveal** the success, happiness, low cost, or other benefits the consumer will get if he or she uses the product. The ads have a **theme**, and use **message unity** (as part of the relate strategy)—design considerations such as the right pictures or visuals, setting, colors, etc. to complete the presentation package. Does this sound familiar?

For those of you who would like more examples of "interpretive" writing using these principles, I recommend reading *Paul Harvey's Rest of the Story*. Here you will find some of the best examples of using Tilden's Tips that I know of, plus it is fun reading.

The Model of Interpretation

In 1977 Gabe Cherem published an article which was (and still is) one of the most significant contributions to the development of a philosophy of interpretation (Cherem, 1977). In this article, Dr. Cherem presented a *Model of Interpretation* to illustrate the "interpretive process" (Figure 6).

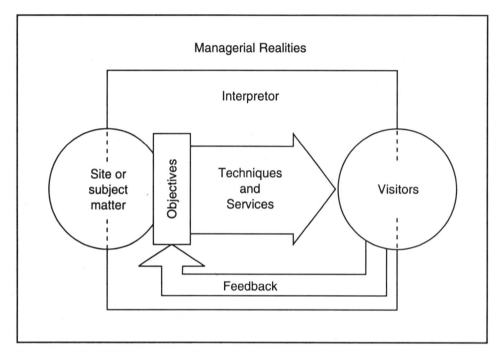

Figure 6. Model of Interpretation (From Cherem, 1977).

Let's take a closer look at this model, and its components. On the left side of the model is a bubble labeled **site or subject matter**—the story to be interpreted. This is WHAT we want to interpret and the main THEME that we will be interpreting.

Next look at the **objectives** box. Before we can create our interpretive message or service, we have to know what we expect to accomplish.

The arrow marked **techniques and services** signifies a number of options for presenting this program or service (live program, self-guided materials, exhibits, etc.). **Techniques** refers to using Tilden's Tips. The **Visitors** portion of the model indicates that we need to have an accurate understanding of who our visitors are, their backgrounds, and motives and expectations for participating in an interpretive program or event.

From the visitors, a **feedback** loop leaves room for evaluation. You will never really know for sure if your program, plan, or service was successful (accomplished its objectives) unless you evaluate the programs or services and visitor response. If the objectives are not accomplished to any degree of satisfaction you had set, you must determine whether the objectives were not reasonable, or whether the interpretive techniques were inappropriate. You may need to revise your objectives, modify your techniques, or try another approach.

The small box around the center elements of the model (**Interpretor**), is you! Every interpretor brings to the planning, design, and presentation of interpretive messages his or her own unique background, experiences, personality, and communication style.

The large box that surrounds everything is called **Managerial Realities**. These are all of the events or circumstances that may have an impact on the planning, design, or development of any given program or service. This include such things as: budget, time constraints, staffing limitations or availability, contracting procedures, availability of materials or resource people, and so on.

To complete the interpretive process, I have added one final consideration to the chapters ahead—**Implementation and Operations** (I&O for short). This includes what it will cost—in time, resources, and money—to implement and operate any plan, program, or service. The model of interpretation presented here forms the basis for the Interpretive Master Planning process I use in developing interpretive plans for everything, from interpretive system plans, master plans, site plans, individual interpretive service (such as a self-guiding trail) plans, and program planning. The following chapters explain how this process is applied to each type of interpretive planning.

References

Cherem, Gabriel J. 1977. "The professional interpretor: Agent for an awakening giant." *Association of Interpretive Naturalists Journal.* 2(1), August.

Lewis, William J. 1988. *Interpreting for Park Visitors.* Eastern National Park & Monument Association. PA.

Tilden, Freeman. 1957. *Interpreting Our Heritage.* The University of North Carolina Press, Chapel Hill.

Veverka, J.A. 1988. *U.S. Army Corps of Engineers Interpretive Services Manual.*

Veverka, J.A. 1990. *Interpretive Master Planning.* John Veverka & Associates, Training Manual.

Chapter Three

The Interpretive Planning Process

It's easy to come up with new ideas; the hard part is letting go of what worked for you two years ago, but will soon be out-of date.

Planning for Interpretive Planning

The Offensive Planner

Basically, I believe that there are two types of planning (and planners). The most common planning that occurs is "defensive" planning. That means that problems have already occurred and the planning is a sort of "damage control" to fix things, to make them right. Lee Iacocca is a good example of an defensive planner. He took over Chrysler with all of its problems and developed plans to get out of trouble.

An "offensive" planner (and plan) looks to anticipate anything that might go wrong after the plan has been implemented. This may include such considerations as:

- Will our visitors change over time (more demands on our resource, want different kinds of interpretive or recreation opportunities, change use patterns, etc.)?
- Will we have enough support (administrative and public), and an adequate budget to implement the plan?

- Will parking areas for the visitor center be able to handle demand a few years from now? Is there ample room for expansion, for school buses, etc.
- Can we locate self-guiding interpretive services (such as trails) close to where the visitors are? It's always a good idea to put new interpretive services as close to current high-use areas as possible, such as campgrounds, picnic areas, and beaches.

In developing an interpretive plan, ask yourself, "What is it that I want this plan to accomplish? How do I intend to use the planning document?" The answers to these questions will dictate, in part, the look, outline, and direct content of the plan. Here are a few uses for an interpretive master plan for a park, forest, historic site, or other location.

Management of the Resources

The interpretive plan could detail how the site or agency's management objectives would be carried out, as well as how interpretive resources could be managed for a variety of uses such as preservation, multiple-use, research, and demonstration areas.

Management and Marketing for Visitors

In planning interpretive programs and services for the site or agency, the marketing plan would look at who is using the site or facilities, demographics, use patterns, and other visitation trends. It would look at ways to improve marketing for the site, how to find new markets, how to advertise and where, and how to increase visitation in general. The interpretive plan can also be used as a funding tool, for grant writing, or other fund raising activities.

Marketing Interpretation Within the Parent Organization

In this case, the interpretive plan will provide supporting strategies to illustrate the services that interpretation can provide to other divisions within the parent agency, and how interpretation can be used as a management tool to help everyone within the agency accomplish the organization's main mission. In addition, it can facilitate the development of possible cooperative relationships with other organizations.

The Planning Team

There is nothing more dangerous than having only one good idea! If nothing else, the one thing I have learned over the past twenty years is the value of tapping into the imagination and creativity of others. Thus, in developing an interpretive plan, it is important to consider who will be involved with the planning project. Here are some basic guidelines for who should be on the planning team. Of course, you should feel free to design your planning team based on the needs of your particular project.

- **Project or Team Leader.** This person is responsible for making the plan happen. He or she would develop the outline for the plan's content and project timeline, and be the interpretive expert for the project. The leader is the ultimate writer or editor for the final planning document.

- **Supervisory Staff Member.** Depending on how a given organization is set up, I think that it is generally good to have on the team the person who wields ultimate power of approval for the finished interpretive plan. That way he or she knows what is going on from the start, and the plan is sure to reflect the issues they feel are important. While the supervisor may not be involved in all aspects of the planning process, he or she should be a part of key meetings and decision points (such as approving objectives, themes, etc.).

- **Support Staff.** Support staff can be brought whenever their involvement is appropriate. The input from biologists, archaeologists, historians, recreation specialists, and so on will provide you with the essential fact base materials needed to develop the theme and objectives for interpretation. They should also be considered to review the plan drafts to make sure the content presentation is correct, and to ensure that recommended interpretive services at select sites (such as in sensitive habitats or at archaeological sites) will not harm the site.

At the very beginning of the planning process, the project leader should detail precisely what everyone's role in the planning process is envisioned to be, and lay out the total project timeline. Set dates for meetings in advance if possible, to ensure that all appropriate team members can fit the meetings to their schedules. Also agree upon review time (one or two weeks) for drafts to help keep the project on schedule.

An Interpretive Planning Model

There are lots of models for planning. The one that I have chosen to use and develop over the past twenty years is based on the Peart/Woods (1976) interpretive planning model (Figure 7). (Note that this model depicts the *planning* process, as distinguished from the interpretive process modeled in Chapter Two.) I like this model for several reasons:

- It's easy to use.
- It covers all the bases.
- It can be used for planning major projects or one interpretive trail sign.
- It works!

The six basic elements of the Interpretive Planning Model are shown in Figure 7 below.

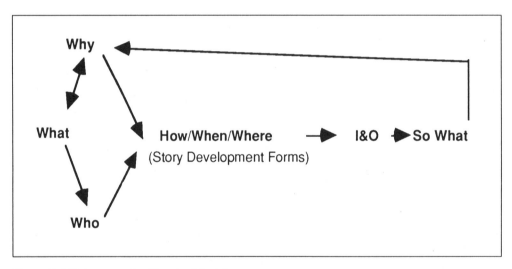

Figure 7. JVA Interpretive Planning Model.

Notice that the Model of Interpretation presented in Chapter Two is very similar to our planning model. Using this model in developing an interpretive plan, the following elements are considered:

WHAT - The resources, theme, and sub-theme to be interpreted.
WHY - The specific objectives that interpretation should accomplish.
WHO - The visitors to our site. How can we relate our theme to them?
HOW/WHEN/WHERE - The presentation of our interpretive programs and services.
I&O - What it will cost (time, resources, budget, people) to implement the various aspects of the plan.
SO WHAT - How we will evaluate the parts of the plan to see if all objectives are being achieved.

Developing Interpretive Master Plans

As you will see, this planning framework can be used for planning everything, from a complete site interpretive master plan, to the planning for one wayside exhibit. Let's take a closer look at each of these sections by walking through them as if we were developing a interpretive master plan for a park, forest, historic site, or other agency or facility.

Look at the project time line for developing an interpretive plan (Figure 8). You will notice that the "front end" of the plan happens concurrently.

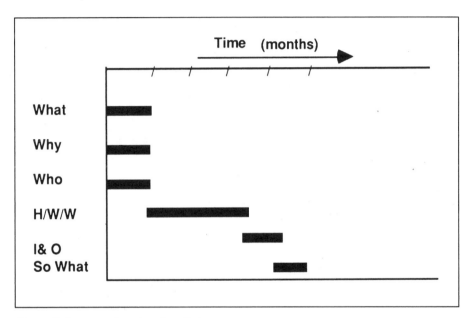

Figure 8. Interpretive plan time line.

The Interpretive Plan Outline

To begin the interpretive planning process, every planner should have a basic outline of the items to be discussed in the plan. Here is a basic interpretive plan outline that I have been using for the past few years. Of course, this outline can be modified to relate to the content or specific needs of your individual plan. Again, note from the project time line above that many parts of the process happen concurrently.

Interpretive Plan General Outline

I. Table of Contents

II. Introduction

III. WHY
   A. Philosophy, policies, goals, and objectives of the agency and for the interpretive plan.
   B. Administrative structure (optional)
   C. Scope of Work/Scope of the Plan

IV. WHAT
   A. Conduct an inventory of all interpretive resources, using the site inventory form:
      1. Site location (note on site index map).
      2. Site description
      3. Seasonal accessibility
      4. Interpretive significance
      5. Include photos, maps, or drawings if appropriate.
   B. Site Index Map
   C. Generate Main Interpretive Theme and Supporting Sub-themes.

V. WHO
   A. Determine demographic characteristics of your visitors.
   B. Isolate specific target groups.
   C. Consider visitor motivations, expectation, perceptions.
   D. Consider visitor orientation systems (pre-visit, on site, post-visit).
   E. Consider any visitor use patterns (time of visit, seasons, etc.).

VI. HOW/WHEN/WHERE
   For each resource inventoried, consider (using story development forms):
   A. Interpretive theme for each individual site.
   B. Site objectives.
   C. Interpretive program objectives.
   D. Recommended interpretive media/services.
   E. Justification
   F. General planner comments.

VII. I&O: Implementation and Operations
   A. Phasing strategy, budgets, staffing needs, etc.

VIII. SO WHAT
   A. Evaluation strategies that could be used to see if the interpretive objectives are being accomplished.

IX. Bibliography and appendices

With the basic interpretive plan outline in hand, let's take a closer look at the content for each section of an interpretive plan.

The WHAT Section

I usually begin my planning process with a thorough inventory of all of the major interpretive resources of the park, forest, or site. The inventory is important in that it helps develop the main theme that the site is best suited to interpret. I look to see what the site is illustrating via its resources, and I write the theme that best summarizes the essence or main story of the site. To help record the resources of the site, I have developed a standard planning form for Resource Inventory (Figure 9).

What Do We Inventory?

When I do an inventory of interpretive resources, I look for:

Biological Areas:

- lakes
- rivers
- habitat types
- unique features
- rare or endangered species
- seasonal events (wildflower blooms, bird migrations, etc.)
- existing or potential demonstration areas
- wildlife management areas/programs
- habitat restoration areas
- timber management areas (type of management)

Cultural Resources:

- old cabin or fort sites.
- old building ruins (sawmills, etc.).
- battlefields
- site of a historic event
- archaeological sites
- old CCC camp sites

Geological Resources:

- bed rock outcrops
- fossil beds
- geological features

Interpretive Site Inventory		Page of

Site Index No:	Site Name:

Site Location:

Site Description:

Seasonal Accessibility:

Interpretive Significance:

Attach photograph/illustration here.

Figure 9.

Existing or Planned Trails or Auto Tours (T-1, or AT-1).

Sensory Areas:

- herb garden
- barnyard
- scenic vistas
- waterfalls

Facilities:

- interpretive or visitor centers
- bridges
- gift shop
- information offices
- kiosks
- demonstration facilities (i.e. sugar bush site).
- farm or homestead

Orientation Areas:

- any nearby attractions, sites, or resources that may not be part of our agency or site, but that may be interpreting the same or related topics.
- key locations for visitor orientation such as major road intersections, campgrounds, boat launch areas, and other prime visitor contact areas.

I assign each resource being inventoried a Site Index Number which will appear on the Inventory sheet, all Story Development Forms, and on a master Site Index Map. Each resource has a letter prefix, such as B for biological sites or C for cultural sites, and a number. So if we have five cultural sites inventoried, they would be coded C-1, C-2, C-3, and so on. See the completed site inventory form (Figure 10) and site index map (Figure 11) from a past planning project on pages 38 and 39. Note that most of the interpretive sites were biological sites (B-1, etc.).

The site index map provides other useful information as well. After the inventory has been completed and mapped, we can see:

- Access routes (or lack of them) to get visitors to various interpretive resources or sites.
- Any potential linking of sites (for large parks, forests, etc.) for developing self-guiding auto tours.
- Any duplication of interpretive sites.
- Potential for distributing visitor flow and use of under-used areas.
- Potential conflict with other sites (recreation areas, archaeological areas, sites or features that need some kind of special management or protection).
- General visitor flow to and through the area, park, forest, or site.
- Potential bottleneck areas or other flow problems.

| Site Index No: B-5 | Site Name: Fire Zone |

Site Location:

The NE section of Price Nature Center, SE¼, NW¼, Sec. 30
T 11 N, R 5 E. Also refer to map on page <u>14</u> of this section.

Site Description:

This is the area of the nature center north of the drainage
ditch. While the fire occurred in 1966, some evidence of
it can still be seen today by way of scars at the bases of
some trees in the area.

Seasonal Accessibility:

Once the trail through this area is developed, visitors to
Price Nature Center could have access to this area all year.
The trail could be used for cross-country skiing in the
winter months, and used for interpretive programs all year
long.

Interpretive Significance:

This site is significant in that it can be utilized to interpret an important aspect of forest ecology, that of the
effects on the forest when a fire occurs, and of the
recovery process. Aspects of fire safety and fire prevention
could also be interpreted in this area.

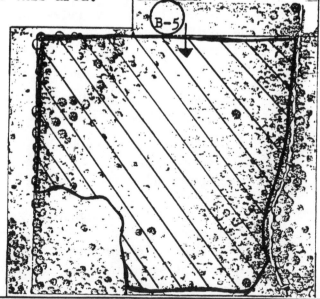

This map illustrates the
approximate area burned
in the fire which occurred
in 1966. About 30 acres
were burned.

Figure 10.

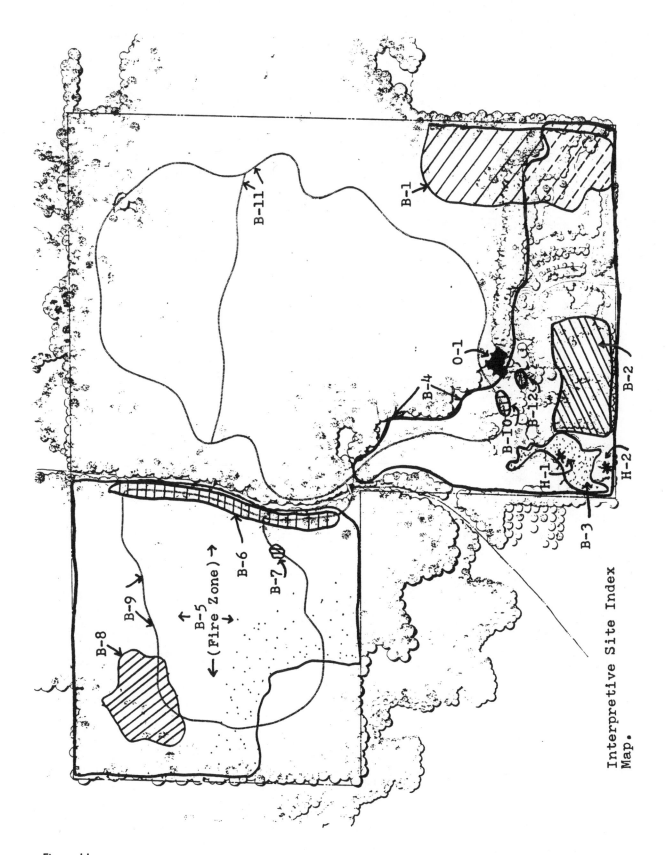

Interpretive Site Index Map.

Figure 11.

How do we do the resource inventory?

There are several techniques for doing the interpretive site resource inventory. The easiest way is to assemble a team of resource specialists (if you have any within your particular organization) and, with a site map in hand, ask each to identify and locate the major interpretive resources (based on the topics presented earlier). Locate each resource on the site map. Then go on-site and look at each one first-hand to make your determination as to its suitability for interpretation (is it a major resource?). If you don't have a resource staff (or *you* are the sole resource staff), you have to go out and walk or drive the areas and make the inventory assessment yourself. For smaller sites, you can take a site topographic map of your area and walk through the whole site, noting on the map the locations of interpretive resources.

Again, for each major resource of some interpretive significance, note its location on the map with a site index number, and complete a Site Inventory form for each resource. Be sure to take a picture of each site for the planning forms. A picture is worth a thousand words!

Interpretive Theme Development

Once you have conducted a thorough inventory of what your site has to offer, you can then develop a main **theme** for the interpretation of the site. The theme should be based on what you actually have on-site.

WHAT is a Theme?

A *theme* is the central or key idea of any presentation. When a good presentation has been completed, the audience should be able to summarize it in one sentence. This sentence would be the theme. Development of a theme provides organizational structure and clarity of understanding. Once the theme has been determined, everything else tends to fall into place. Themes should:

- Be stated as complete sentences.
- Contain one main idea.
- Reveal the overall purpose of the presentation.
- Be stated in an interesting manner.

Once you have your main theme, then select those resources on-site for interpretation that best illustrate that theme. Here is a sample of interpretive themes from a 1993 Forest Service Interpretive Master Planning Course. These are themes for different forest districts in Utah.

- The history of Logan Canyon is one of relationships between human need and natural resources.
- The multiple use of the Forest benefits people and wildlife.
- Hidden within the scenic beauty is a multitude of conservation and Forest management practices that enhance the Forest experience.

Now these themes are what I like to call "Big Picture" themes. They tend to be more general—they cover a larger story. Program themes can be more specific. Here are program or service (such as self-guiding trail) theme examples.

- Exploring caves is a sensuous experience.
- Mosquitos are fascinating insects.
- Geyser function is dependent on three variables.
- The grizzly's survival is threatened.
- Lincoln's life was often marred by tragedy.
- We are using three different management techniques to improve wildlife habitats.
- There are many ways you can help protect this historic park.
- The zoo animals need your help.

Check your theme. When you have written your theme, you shouldn't have to ask the question, "What about it?" after you hear it. For example, is this a theme? "Birds of the Park."

"What about 'Birds of the Park," you ask? What will the program actually be about? To change this topic to a real theme we could re-write it to be "Our unique land management programs help protect migratory song birds that nest in the park." With this theme, it is easy to see what the program will be about and what kinds of things will need to be illustrated.

One way to look at the relationships between the theme for the whole site and interpretation of sub-themes using a varity of media or services is shown in Figure 12.

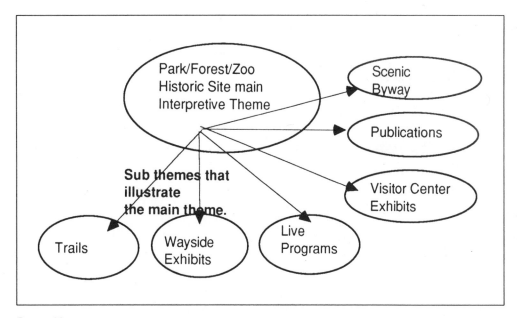

Figure 12.

With the above example, the main interpretive theme might be "The park is using a variety of innovative land management techniques to restore damaged habitats."

With this main theme, each of the on-sites service (such as self-guiding trails) would be used to illustrate just how and what innovative techniques are actually being done. Visitors can see them first-hand. So a sub-theme for a self-guiding trail might be "The Upland Discovery Trail illustrates how three kinds of reforestation programs are improving habitat for wildlife."

One way to assess your main interpretive theme is by filling in the blank in the following statement.

After the visitors have spent the day (or days, a week) at our site, walked our trails, attended programs, viewed exhibits, etc., and they are in their cars ready to return home, if they only remember one thing after all they have seen or done, by gosh, that one thing they better absolutely remember is........................ !
The answer will probably be your main theme.

As another example, here is one theme and sub-theme strategy that a zoo might develop (Figure 13).

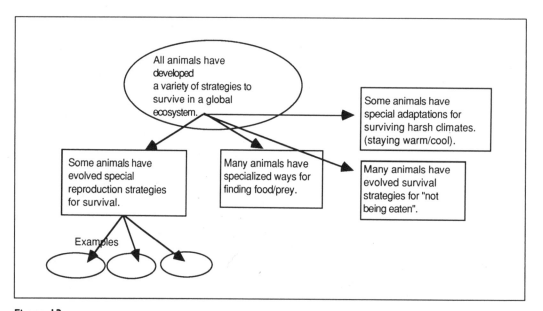

Figure 13.

In this example, the objective is for all visitors to be aware of how different animals have evolved strategies to survive. Thus, each zoo animal would illustrate one or more of these concepts or sub themes. The important thing to notice here is that we have taken the emphasis away from the "name" of the animal and its general natural history, and focused on the survival strategy the animal illustrates. That doesn't mean we don't provide the name, but it's just not very important for visitors to learn.

Why this Approach?

This theme structure for the zoo example brings out the main purpose of interpretation. First of all, most visitors could care less about the "scientific name" of the animal, and will almost as quickly forget the common name of unfamiliar animals. Given the fact that they will see perhaps a hundred different animals during their visit, they simply cannot remember that many names. While there are reasons for having scientific names on animal signs at zoos, we must remember that a "scientific" name is really a common name in a dead language (Latin) that visitors have no need for. Secondly, most visitors have no use for, or reason to remember, all of the natural history baggage we load upon these kinds of signs. Unless you have a hippopotamus living in your backyard, you probably don't care too much about how much it eats or its gestation period. **Many of these signs are giving visitors answers to questions nobody is asking!** Perhaps we should take some time to find out what sort of information visitors do find interesting and what will help them value all of the animals that they are viewing and learning about.

What's Important Here?

In the WHY section that follows we will look at what objectives individual interpretive services are to accomplish, and what is really important for visitors to know or feel. Is it really important for visitors to be able to name all of the zoo animals, or is it perhaps more important for them to understand that all animals have value, and are at risk due to habitat loss? Which concept or theme is the most important to interpret? Which will have the most impact in helping protect and conserve habitats?

The main goal of planning the theme is to help us focus on exactly what—given limited money, time, and other resources—we want our interpretation to communicate to our visitors. What is our story, our "big picture"? After the visitors leave the park, zoo, forest, historic site, or facility, the theme is the ONE THING they better be able to remember or understand as a result of the time spent with you.

The WHY Section

Developing Interpretive Missions Statements, Goals, and Objectives

WHERE ARE WE GOING? That is the question answered by the development of interpretive mission statements, goals, and objectives. We cannot do interpretive planning (or any kind of planning for that matter) without a sense of mission and clear goals and objectives.

Mission Statements

I usually recommend developing the interpretive services (or site/facility) mission statement after the resource inventory and theme/sub-theme development. The reason for this is that if you write the mission statement before you know what you have to interpret (your theme or story), then the mission statement—and not the resources (stuff you actually have on-site to interpret)—will drive the interpretation. You may find yourself trying to force a story onto a site or facility that may not be appropriate for it.

What is a *mission statement*? A mission statement should state, in concise terms, three things: 1) who you are; 2) what you do; and 3) why you do it. Here is an example of a "generic" mission statement.

> *It is the mission of the (your site name here) to interpret to all visitors using a variety of innovative and creative interpretive services, the theme (put your theme here), and to facilitate an enjoyable and safe recreational learning experience for all site visitors, while instilling and demonstrating positive land use ethics in all site programs and management activities.*

The mission statement gives the overall direction for interpretive services, and all programs and services will have, as an objective, the task of helping to accomplish the mission statement.

Interpretive Goals and Objectives

The development of goals and objectives is the key to success for any interpretive plan. They provide the direction and content of all interpretive services.

Interpretive goals - Goals are a general statement of things that you would like to have happen, but aren't very specific, or measurable. Some examples of interpretive goals for an overall site interpretive plan might include:

- To have a visitor-friendly orientation system for the site.
- To have a variety of interpretive programs and services aimed at different market groups.
- To conduct a visitor analysis or survey program for the site.
- To develop a marketing plan for the site.

In general, I don't spend too much time working on goals, but rather spend time in developing the specific objectives an interpretive plan is to accomplish.

What are Interpretive Objectives - Objectives are measurable. Either you accomplished them, or you didn't! Here are a few examples of interpretive objectives for an interpretive master plan for a park.

- All visitors will be able to easily find all of the park's facilities upon entering park property.
- The majority of the visitors will be able to state, in concept, the main interpretive theme of the site after interacting with interpretive programs and services offered during their visit.
- After attending park interpretive programs, the majority of visitors will be able to state five ways we are using state-of-the-art conservation practices to improve habitats for wildlife and people.
- By the end of their visit, the majority of visitors will learn and remember which agency is responsible for the management of this park.
- The majority of visitors will understand how the historical events recreated at our site illustrate the efforts of African Americans to end slavery in the United States.

What Kinds of Objectives Do We Use for Developing Interpretive Plans at Any Level?

Over the past few years I have been using three basic kinds of objectives in developing interpretive master plans for parks, forests, and other sites. These three kinds of objectives include:

- Learning Objectives
- Behavioral Objectives
- Emotional Objectives

Let's take a closer look at each of these.

Learning Objectives

(What you want the visitors to learn or remember.)

These are the most commonly used objectives and focus on visitors being able to name, list, describe, illustrate, etc., desired items upon completion of any given program or service, or, in the case of an interpretive master plan, upon leaving the site. Examples of learning objectives include:

- The majority of visitors will be able to list five ways the forest is using state-of-the-art conservation techniques to improve habitats for wildlife.
- The majority of visitors will be able to describe the four main steps in making iron in a nineteenth century iron furnace.
- The majority of visitors will be able to list three survival strategies illustrated by the birds on display in the nocturnal wildlife exhibit.

Behavioral Objectives

(What you want the visitors to do.)

These are, in my opinion, the most important of the objectives. These are the ones that help focus on what it is that you want the visitors to do (how you want them to use the information you are giving them). They are the "pay-off" objectives, and for most managers, they are the "results" of interpretive programs and services. Some examples of behavioral objectives include:

- The majority of visitors will want to try at least one new (learned) conservation technique to attract wildlife to their home by the end of this year.
- The majority of visitors will treat all of our site resources with a sense of respect and stewardship.
- The majority of visitors will take recommended safety measures before attempting to hike the "Trail of No Return" interpretive trail.
- The majority of visitors will not feed any zoo animals.
- The majority of visitors will want to join in local efforts for historical preservation.

Emotional Objectives

(You can't begin to change or alter behavior or attitudes unless you accomplish these.)

Emotional objectives are the "driving force" objectives. These are the ones that help visitors to remember the topic because of a strong "feeling" they create in the visitor, and are instrumental in helping to accomplish the behavioral objectives. They help the visitor to feel surprise, anger, sadness, guilt, acceptance, pride, and other desired emotions related to the subject matter. Here are some emotional objectives.

- By the time they are ready to leave the site, the majority of visitors will feel that taking an active role in recycling materials at home helps people and wildlife; they will feel "good" about recycling.
- The majority of visitors will be surprised and amazed to see how the forest landscape has changed since being totally logged over in the 1920s to become the lush, green landscape they see today.
- The majority of visitors will feel a sense of pride that this historic resource has been preserved to illustrate the citizens' heroic actions here during the Civil War.

Here are other examples of learning, emotional, and behavioral objectives for an exhibit on littering.

- The majority of visitors will be able to describe how long it takes a piece of paper, an aluminum can, a piece of gum, and a plastic cup to biodegrade.
- The majority of visitors who currently are not concerned about littering, will not litter anymore.
- The majority of visitors will pick up other litter they may see on the ground and throw it in trash cans.
- The majority of visitors will feel that litter is a disgusting habit that produces an unclean and undesirable place for them and their children to visit.
- The majority of visitors will feel that there is "no excuse" to litter.

Can you spot the different kinds of objectives used in this example? Managers could probably care less if visitors can list how long it takes things to biodegrade. If visitors learn this, and still litter, all you have is well-educated litterers. The main objectives for the manager are the behavioral ones.

Levels of Objectives

When you are developing an interpretive plan for an entire park, zoo, historic site, forest, or other facility, you will need to develop several levels of objectives. These will include the overall objectives for the whole place, the things that all interpretive programs and services are directed to accomplish. Next come the specific objectives that each interpretive site (demonstration area, self-guiding trail, auto tour, individual historic sites, etc.) is to accomplish. And after that comes program objectives, which are even more specific and detailed, such as those you would develop for each stop on a self-guiding tour.

Figure 14 illustrates the hierarchy of interpretive objectives, as they are related to your mission.

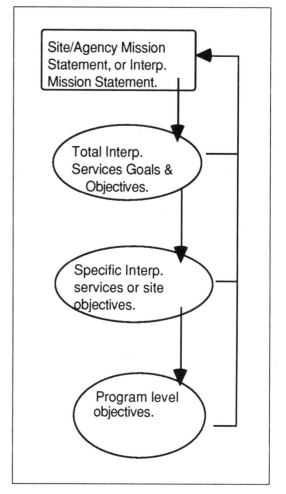

Figure 14. The hierarchy of interpretive objectives.

Figure 15 provides a more detailed example with one objective written for each level of presentation. Notice that as we go from a site, park, or forest-wide interpretive objective we get more and more specific as to what the interpretation should accomplish.

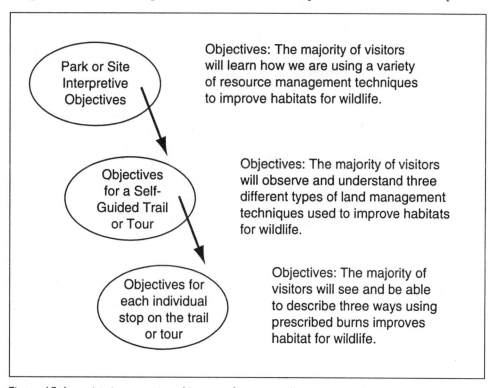

Figure 15. Layering interpretive objectives from overall site to specific stops on an interpretive trail.

The Two MOST Important Questions a Planner Has to Ask and Answer!

As I begin to develop objectives at any level, there are two questions that I always ask myself, and I recommend them for you, too.

The first question is, "WHY would a visitor want to know that?"

Are we giving answers to questions that nobody is asking? If you, as a planner, cannot answer this question about any objective you are developing, you have a problem. Remember: if a visitor has no reason to know or learn the information we want to present, two things will probably happen. One, the visitor will not come to the program or activity, or will not remember the information from an exhibit. And second, the visitor will probably forget the information almost immediately after encountering it. Always plan to use interpretive principles and techniques to **provoke** curiosity and interest, and to **relate** the material to the everyday life of the viewer. If there isn't some obvious reason for the visitors to want to learn this information, you have to "create" a reason for them.

The second question is, "How do I want the visitors to use the information I am giving them?"

If you don't want the visitors to use the information being interpreted to them, then why are you giving it to them?

Remember Our Discussion on Behavioral Objectives?

Think back to Chapter One where I mentioned that visitors remember 10 percent of what they hear, 30 percent of what they read, 50 percent of what they see, and 90 percent of what they do. This is another important consideration for developing your behavioral objectives. For example, every interpretive sign, wayside exhibit panel, or other outdoor exhibit should always encourage visitors to DO something. They should be directed in the text to: look for..., see if you can find..., can you see the..., touch the bark on the tree in front of you, feel how heavy...., etc. Not only are the behavioral objectives the "pay-off" objectives, but they are also key in helping the visitors to REMEMBER activities, concepts, and experience.

THIS IS VERY IMPORTANT TO REMEMBER! (Think of something to DO to help you remember this point, like write it down or highlight it with a yellow marker!)

Other Reasons for Objectives—Cost Per Visitor Contact and Cost Effectiveness

Working with clear objectives in mind is also important for several other reasons, and chief among them is the usefulness of objectives in evaluating interpretive programs and services. We will talk more about evaluation later in this chapter, but here are some things to begin thinking about.

There are "business" aspects to objectives as well. They can help save your interpretive programs in times of tight budgets, or help you get more funding to try new programs or services. One way this works is to show the "return" (objectives that are met) the agency is getting from presenting the program or service. For example, we can actually calculate the total cost of a program per visitor contact. Add up all of the costs for planning and presenting any given program, exhibit, trail, brochure, etc., and divide that cost by the number of visitors who use that service. If it costs $4,000 for a wayside exhibit panel, and 40,000 visitors each year see and learn from that panel, the cost per visitor contact (given a use life of five years) would be $4,000 divided by 200,000, or a cost per contact of about two cents.

Now, while this is a very low cost per contact, the question is, "What are we getting in return for our cost per contact? This is where the objectives come in. If 70 percent of the objective(s) for the sign are being accomplished, then the sign is cost effective. That is, you are getting "something" in return for the investment. But if you find out that only 2 percent of the objective(s) are being accomplished (or that 98 percent of the visitors aren't learning anything at all), then the exhibit is not cost effective.

Here is another example. Let's say that you plan, design, and present over the course of a season (four months) a program with an objective to have people not litter. Lets also say for the sake of this example, that last year your agency spent $2,000 on picking up litter. Now, lets say that your program cost $1,000 to plan, design, and present over the four-month season, and that at the end of this current year, the cost for litter pick up for your agency was only $500 for the entire year. Now assume for the sake of this example that the only difference between this year and last year was YOUR program against litter. Let's also assume that 5,000 visitors attended your program over the course of the season.

Now we can determine that your cost per contact for this program this season was $1,000 divided by 5,000 visitors, or twenty cents per visitor contact. Now what did you get for your twenty cents? The total program cost $1,000 to put on, but the program SAVED the agency $1,500 in litter pick up costs. So the program actually "made" $500 (the difference from the program cost and the savings to the agency). In other words, the program made ten cents per visitor contact, and is a very cost-effective program. But besides the cost savings, it also freed up other people and budget for other jobs!

Of course not all programs will be able to show a benefit like this, especially if we are trying to accomplish emotional or other types of objectives. You will have to determine what will constitute a cost-effective result for each particular situation.

What you gain when you take this "business approach" to interpretation is evidence that your programs (and budget) are indeed benefiting the agency as well as your visitors, and that they are cost effective. Who else in your agency is doing that?

The WHO Section

An Analysis of Your Market (Visitors) for Interpretive Planning

Another important aspect of developing an interpretive plan is to conduct an analysis of who your market or potential visitors are. The more you learn about who your visitors are, where they are coming from, and their motives and expectations for their visit with you, the better you can design programs or services (present your story) to **relate** to their particular interests and needs.

There are also two levels of visitor analysis. Level one is doing a thorough visitor or market analysis in developing an interpretive plan for your site. This is to help you plan for all of your programs and services. You should look at visitor flow into, through, and out of your site; the numbers of visitors you might expect; seasonal uses; etc. The second level of visitor analysis is more for the specific interpretive program or service level. Within your general market base of visitors, try to determine who might use a specific program, such as a guided hike, or who of all your site visitors might be most interested in learning about the theme you are presenting. Examples of these market groups might be: school groups of fifth graders, a garden club, elderly visitors from a bus tour, a 4-H club, and so on. Who do you think the user group for a self-guided trail through your site might be?

This section focuses on doing a market (visitor) analysis for an Interpretive Master Plan for an entire facility. See chapters Four, Five, and Six for ideas about doing a market analysis for specific programs and services.

Visitor Demographics

Looking at visitor demographics is a good first step when doing a visitor analysis because these are often some of the easiest data to collect. A study of visitor demographics should reveal:

- Where visitors are coming from.
- Age groups and sex of visitors.
- Socio-economic background.
- Use patterns.

What will this information tell you? Knowing where visitors are coming from (regional or counties, cities, etc.) gives you information on advertising or promoting your programs or services (assuming you want to promote the programs). It also tells you where visitors are NOT coming from. You can identify where to increase your marketing to attract new or different market groups. By learning where visitors travel from to get to the site, you can also make assumptions about travel routes and better plan highway directional signs to the site. This also helps in developing maps or directions for visitors. Of course, learning who is NOT visiting your site may be as important as knowing who IS coming to your site.

Demographics about age groups and group composition also helps in planning programs and services. For example, if you find that mostly older populations visit your site, you may need to plan special accommodations (barrier-free access, benches, etc.) for older visitors in campgrounds, visitor centers, restrooms, and on interpretive trails. Remember that different age groups of visitors have different expectations for their visits to different sites, and look for different amenities or mixes of recreational and interpretive opportunities.

If you have an existing site, **unobtrusive evaluation** offers an easy way to find out who your visitors are. You can then compare this profile with the kind of visitor mix you desire. In general you will have one or more of the following "groups" using your site or facility:

- Traditional family (mom, dad, children)
- Traditional extended family (mom, dad, kids, grandparents or other relatives)
- Single parent with children (one of the fastest growing user groups).
- Adult groups without children (young couples)
- "Empty Nesters" (Adults usually in their late 40s or so who have grown children who are in college or out of the house on their own).
- Elderly or retired visitors (visitors over age 65 traveling either as couples or as groups in organized tours).

These are the main categories I use in evaluation, but you can add any group category to this as appropriate for your site, such as hunters (seasonal use), etc. To find out who your main user groups are, stake out a staff member or volunteer in a parking area or at the park or site entrance with a checklist of these categories on it. As a vehicle comes by or visitors exit their vehicles in parking areas, check the category that each "group" looks like it best fits into. Within a week or so (be sure you survey during weekends), you will begin to see a profile emerge of your visitor mix. This will give you some ideas about how to best relate your theme, etc. to each different market group. It will also help guide you toward the types of programs and services these visitors may be most interested in.

Visitation use patterns allow you to see when your site and services are most in demand. I recommend that you graph your weekly or monthly visitor attendance figures for each year. By graphing the data, you can see any patterns of use, or seasonal anomalies in use. Here are a number of examples from visitor surveys from some of my past projects that show how to present and analyze this kind of visitor use data.

Figure 16 illustrates an easy way to obtain and display some kinds of visitor data. For this project I recorded the counties of origin for each car in the park's parking lot (the counties' names were printed on each license plate). Then after the survey time, I counted the number from each county and put the number in a state-wide county map. How would you use this information?

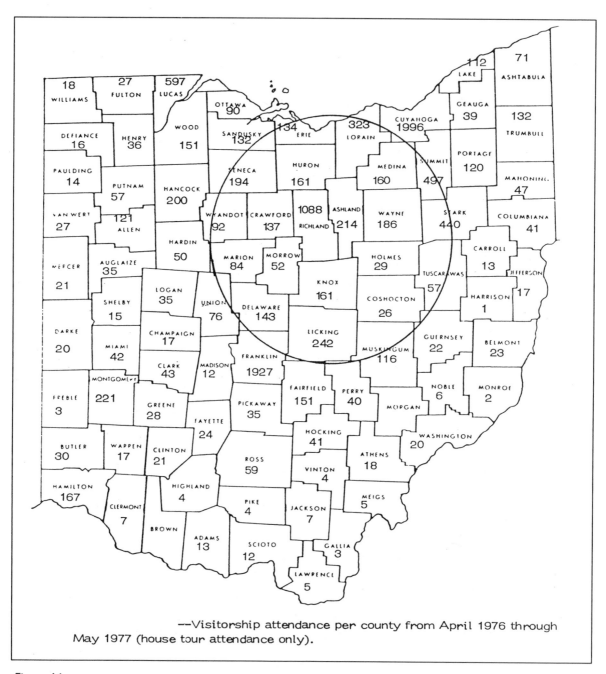

—Visitorship attendance per county from April 1976 through May 1977 (house tour attendance only).

Figure 16.

Figure 17 is from another project where I graphed program attendance from the past two years. Graphing data really helps to point out any anomalies or use patterns. Note the "spike" in the attendance curve for May, which does not occur the following year. Why do you think that spike occurred? (The site had a special spring wildflower program that year that brought in lots of people.)

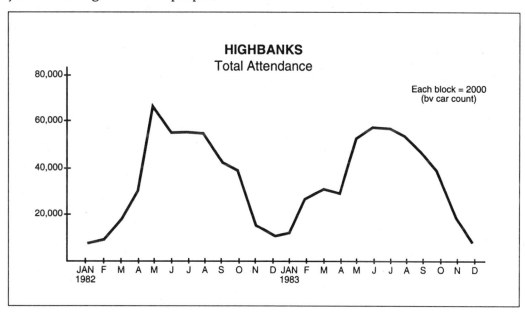

Figure 17.

Figure 18 illustrates what you can learn if you graph visitor center attendance. I asked the front desk staff to count the number of visitors in this particular center every half hour from the time they opened until they closed that evening, for one week. The resulting graphs give us a picture of use of and demand for the center and center facilities.

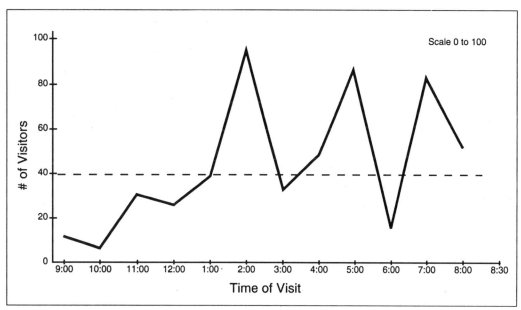

Figure 18.

In the figure of the week-long graph, the dotted line is the *psychological carrying capacity* of the center. That is the point at which visitors, upon looking from the doorway at the number of people inside, decide NOT to go in. By noting the times at which the number of visitors in the facility exceeds the psychological carrying capacity, you can make adjustments in your programs or services to compensate for the peaks. You may decide to add seasonal or volunteer staff, change exhibit flow patterns for a quicker turn around time, or create or promote outside activities to draw off some of the facility demand.

Visitor Motivations for Selecting and Attending Interpretive Programs

In doing visitor analysis for interpretive planning for any site, the traditional kinds of visitor data collected are basically demographics, as discussed earlier. Many years ago when I first got into interpretive research and theory, I was working as a seasonal interpretive naturalist with Ohio State Parks. I felt that our programs were not very well aimed at what visitors might want, and we had been doing essentially the same programs for years. As part of my master's degree program at Ohio State, I developed a research project to try to find out what motivates visitors to select and attend interpretive programs. I was amazed to learn as I was doing my literature search how few people had spent any time thinking about "what the visitors wanted." We were more concerned in planning programs that we—the interpretors—were interested in. The research project really opened my eyes as to how poorly we understood our visitors, and how ineffective we probably were in communicating with them.

The Research Setting

The study I am going to share with you was done many years ago, and the results I present here were valid only for the **time, place, and audience** for which the research was conducted. What this study illustrates is the KINDS of concepts I learned from this research. To my surprise, this was exactly the kind of research that marketing and advertising firms have been doing for years, helping them to plan marketing programs for new or existing products.

The setting was an Ohio State Park. Our visitors were essentially "residents" in the park for a week at a time. They came into the park and settled into their campsites on Sundays usually, and left the following Sunday morning.

The kinds of traditional programs offered at the park were: guided hikes, live demonstrations, and evening slide talks. The average attendance for one of the guided hikes was about 20 people, and the average attendance for our evening slide programs (offered about 9 p.m.) was 350 visitors each evening. The obvious assumption I made was that our visitors preferred the evening programs most, and "loved us" and the topics we presented during these programs.

Visitor Motives

As part of the research I wanted to learn what motivated visitors to attend or select the services or program topics that we offered. To set the research strategy, I based the motives categories on Maslow's (1954) hierarchy of needs. In Chapter One you learned that visitors have a mix of motives or needs for their selections of program or services. These included: physiological needs, safety needs, the need to belong, esteem needs, and the need for self actualization.

The survey was divided into two main information gathering areas. First, I wanted to learn which interpretive services (hikes, live demonstrations, slide talks) visitors preferred, and why. Second, I hoped to find out which program topics visitors most preferred to attend, and why. The choices for program topics were taken from a pre-tested list of thirty topics most commonly offered in the parks at that time.

What did We Learn from the Research?

The results for the kinds of interpretive services preferred by the visitors really surprised me. At my park the most highly attended programs were the evening slide shows (about 350 visitors per night). Our least attended programs were the daily guided hikes. But the research results (Figure 19) show that the visitors actually wanted more hikes, and didn't like our evening slide program. The comments ran something like: "we didn't come to the park to see pictures of wildlife—we came to see the real thing!" So in this case past program attendance alone wasn't a good indicator of success. The main reason, I found, that visitors came to our evening slide programs was because there was nothing else to do in the park at night! Their retention of any of the information from the program itself was very little.

Figure 20 illustrates the stated reasons (motives) that visitors selected either a hike or live demonstration activity. Note that the major motive for hiking was enjoyment, not "learning." When the words "learn" or "educational experience" were dropped from the advertising for hikes, attendance on the hikes increased. Visitors associated "learning" with school or a formal education program. But they were on vacation. They didn't want schooling, they wanted fun.

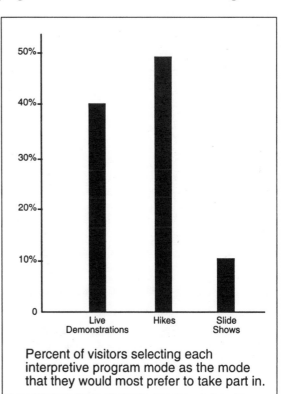

Percent of visitors selecting each interpretive program mode as the mode that they would most prefer to take part in.

Figure 19.

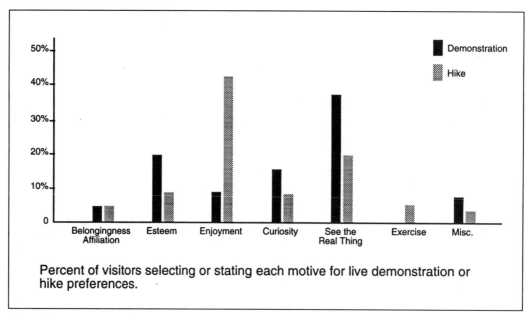

Percent of visitors selecting or stating each motive for live demonstration or hike preferences.

Figure 20.

I also looked at *when* our visitors would prefer to go on guided hikes (Figure 21). Of course the times that they stated in the survey as "preferred" times to go on hikes were not times that we actually offered hikes. It turned out that evenings were a preferred hiking time, so we eliminated most evening slide shows and added evening night hikes. The results were great, as we now offered visitors the interpretive program or activity they liked the best, at times that they liked the best. What a concept for program planning!

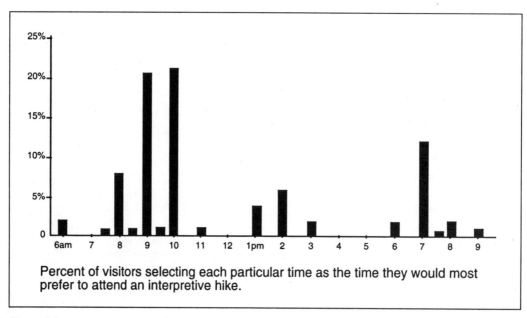

Percent of visitors selecting each particular time as the time they would most prefer to attend an interpretive hike.

Figure 21.

I also learned a few more interesting things about the visitors. While both men and women might prefer a particular program topic, they might prefer it for different reasons. For example, one program topic I surveyed was "Tornadoes and Thunderstorms...the Deadly Clouds." I found that men chose this topic for esteem motives, wanting to learn how deadly the clouds were and how destructive they could be. The men would be up on the roof with a video recorder taping the twister as it went by. The women in the survey selected this topic for safety and the need-to-belong motives. They wanted to learn how to protect their family if a tornado was coming! By not being aware of the diversity in motives involved in visitors' program selection and expectations of what they want to learn, an interpretor could present the program in such a way as to miss half of the audience, leaving them unsatisfied.

What Can You Do With This Kind of Information?

This was just a small part of the total amount of information I learned about the park visitors. Park staff used this information the following year to better plan, design, present, and **market** the interpretive programs. The park eliminated slide programs and made all programs interactive, with hands-on learning opportunities. When we did use slides, it was only as a part of the total program. We offered program topics that were of the most interest to the visitors, and we offered programs at times that the visitors told us was best for them. We also used this data to formulate an advertising strategy. The results were a thirty-seven percent increase in our interpretive program attendance from the past year. We didn't have more new visitors, but we had more visitors attending more programs during their week's stay in the park.

Visitor analysis can also be used to help you estimate potential demand for your site and services. In particular, it is very useful in helping to predict demand for a new visitor center. The example given here is for a park, forest, or site that has existing programs or services (camping, fishing, etc.), but no visitor center. Here is how you can get an idea for estimating potential demand for a new facility.

Design Load for Visitor Centers

Let's look at how to determine or estimate how many people will visit a given facility on an average peak season weekend day or holiday. For the following example it is assumed that 80 percent of visitors will use the center. The design load is determined using the following equation:

$$DL = \frac{VI \times 0.80 \times VS \times VW}{NW}$$

DL= Design load for the visitor center
VI= Total visitation for recreation/interpretive programs (estimate).
VS= Percentage of visitation occurring during your peak season.
VW= Percentage of peak season visitation occurring on weekend days or holidays.
NW= Number of weekend days or holidays during the peak season.

For our example, we will plug in numbers from an actual project.

$$DL = \frac{521,000 \times 0.80 \times 0.80 \times 0.70}{27}$$

$$DL = \frac{233,408}{27} = 8,644$$

To determine the number of People At One Time (PAOT) expected in the visitor center, the following equation is used:

$$\frac{PAOT}{} = \frac{DL}{H \times TR}$$

DL = Design Load from above
H = Number of hours of operation (8 hours used for our example)
TR = Turnover Rate (estimated 20 minutes length of visit or turnover rate of 3 visitors per hour).

$$PAOT = \frac{8644}{8 \times 3} = 360$$

This particular center can expect about 360 visitors at one time on its busiest weekend day during the summer.

Now consider that, if there is 900 square feet of space available in the exhibit area, and the minimum amount of space for comfort for visitors is 16 square feet of space per person, this exhibit area can hold about 56 visitors comfortably at one time. In this case, the building was designed before the math was done (visitor market potential analysis). What potential problems do you see here? What would you do if this was your center, and you were confronted with the above information?

Visitor Orientation Needs

One of the basic needs that visitors have, which relates to Maslow's safety need, is that of orientation. Without good directions (maps, highway signs, etc.) visitors can go through a good deal of trip stress. Many family arguments that occur on vacations are due to difficulty in trying to find the vacation spot. Interpretive planners should strive to reduce trip stress, considering three levels of planning for visitor orientation.

- Pre-visit Orientation
- On-site Visit Orientation
- Post-visit Orientation

Let's take a closer look at what's involved with each of these levels.

Pre-visit orientation involves providing information for visitors on:

- The kinds of programs, services, facilities, and activities you have at your site or facility.
- Hours of operation, costs, seasonal uses, need for reservations, and phone numbers to call for more information.
- A map with directions from main access routes from all directions.
- A system of directional signs off-site guiding them to the site.
- An introduction to the mission and theme of the site or facility.
- Any other information you think they should know to help them understand more about you, or to help "attract" them to you if you are a tourism type site.

On-site orientation involves providing directions to all of your resources, facilities, use areas, parking, and offices once visitors enter your property. It also involves making them aware of programs or services you have available (what, when, and where) for them to use or take part in.

Post-visit orientation involves making sure that visitors can easily find their way back to the highway or main travel route when they leave your site, and that they are aware of future or new programs or services, special events, etc. to encourage them to come back to your site soon for another visit.

This whole visitor orientation package has one main goal: to relieve trip stress for visitors so they can easily find you and enjoy their experience at your site.

Pacing Interpretive Services

The concept of pacing is not new. A great deal of our everyday life is developed around this concept, from our school system to almost any sports or recreation activity we might take part in. Knowing that visitors differ widely in their ages, educational attainment, interests, and goals to be achieved within a leisure setting, the interpretor must be sensitive to all levels of visitor experience and sophistication with regard to program or service offerings.

When visitors attend an interpretive program, they come with different levels of knowledge or information about any given topic, or with different skill levels that they might need to use during a program or activity. So pacing interpretive services simply means that we might try to have program topics presented at different knowledge levels, such as having four different trail guides for one self-guiding trail:

- The children's trail guide (simple and built around children's learning principles and examples).
- The parents' trail guide (written to help parents or teachers help the children see, learn, and explore the trail, with questions to ask, answers, and so on.)
- The general trail guide (written for most visitors).
- The advanced trail guide (written for experts, or visitors who already have a basic understanding of the trail theme and topics and want more details.)

Pacing interpretive services might also mean that we have several different kinds of trail opportunities for visitors, such as:

- Short self-guiding loop trail, barrier free.
- Short self-guiding loop trail, not barrier free.
- Short self-guiding loop trail, rugged terrain, steep slopes.
- Long (1 mile or more) trails, for more experienced hikers.
- Difficult trails (several miles) for experienced hikers.

It's important to have some opportunity for all of our major visitor groups. In general, plan to pace in four main areas:

1. Enjoyment levels of the visitor. Some visitors will enjoy (or expect to enjoy) certain program topics or experiences more than others. Some programs maybe more serious or scientific, others just pure fun.
2. Levels of complexity of information provided at interpretive programs or in interpretive media.
3. Levels of motor skills or skill ability needed for some interpretive services, such as backpacking, day hiking, craft programs, living history activities.
4. Visitor attitude. That is, pacing to modify or encourage visitors to change their attitudes about some kinds of topics or activities (bats, snakes, hunting, conservation practices, land or resource stewardship).

For ease of use of the pacing concept, I like to use three different mastery levels. These include:

Level 1 Introductory level for those with little or no knowledge or experience.

Level 2 A medium level for those with more experience or physical abilities.

Level 3 A top level for those who possess a high degree of mastery, ability, or experience.

One example of these levels might be visitors who have never been on a hike before (level 1); visitors that go hiking only when on their vacations, and only for short day hikes (level 2); and visitors who are experienced backpackers and go out for days at a time (level 3).

In the case of enjoyment and attitude, the planner wouldn't be concerned with "mastery" but rather the "intensity" of the effort directed toward changing or planning around various visitor attitudes or the intensity or amount of humor to be included in planning the interpretive programs or services. This is particularly true when interpreting sensitive issues or topics, such as the effects cattle have on riparian habitats to a group of western ranchers who graze their cattle on public land, or historical interpretation about Native Americans.

One of the most common examples of pacing used today is that of pacing for different age groups. Age must be considered in the overall pacing concept for interpretive services, as mastery levels or topic interests can and often do change with age. For example, from the motivation research project I did with Ohio State Parks, I found that there were specific preferences in program topics that older visitors (age 45 and older) preferred (e. g., "What your family can do to fight against pollution") but drew no interest from younger visitors (14 to 25 years old). There were some program topics that younger audiences preferred (e. g., "Snakes-the deadly hunters!") that the older audiences (45 and up) showed little or no interest in.

Use of Interpretive Pacing by Planners

Of course any one park, forest, or historic site cannot possibly plan to offer too many different levels of interpretive services without first knowing something about the visitors coming to the site. This is one more reason why a visitor analysis is so important to interpretive planning. After a survey is done, you may learn that only one or two levels of pacing are needed. Or, if you have a very diverse audience, a variety of offerings could be planned. There is not a *right* amount of pacing for each site; appropriate pacing depends on your particular audience or visitor characteristics. Pacing is a tool to help plan for visitor needs and to help visitors more fully enjoy their recreational and interpretive opportunities during their visit. It helps you **relate** better to individual visitors or groups of visitors by offering programs or services that best fit their needs or abilities. So, for example, if you have a mostly older market using your park or site, it's probably not a good idea to plan for lots of very long hiking trails, when level 1 or 2 trails would best fit that group.

The first places to look for some basic visitor demographic information for your area include:

- Regional or local Chambers of Commerce. Most have done marketing studies on tourism trends for your region or city.
- Your State Travel and Tourism Bureau. States are always conducting tourism trends and travel studies. Most have research done by regions on tourism interests, travel patterns, regional demographic patterns, seasonal visitation trends, and so on.
- State office for the U.S. Census Bureau. The U.S. Census Bureau has a wealth of information available about almost every city, county, or region of the United States. The bureau can give you specific information about visitors and residents in your city or area.

Summary

In this section I could not go into all the aspects of conducting a market survey, but rather chose to demonstrate that you *need* a market survey to help you more effectively plan for meeting your visitors' needs and expectations. If you need help in developing a survey, you may want to contact a local university's Parks and Recreation Department, or Marketing Department. They can provide you with detailed references on how to do a formal survey. They might even have a student looking to do this kind of survey research for his or her thesis. Interpretive consulting firms can also help you conduct research. Remember, to better plan for and interpret to visitors in a truly professional manner...we need to first know who our visitors are!

HOW/WHEN/WHERE
To Plan, Design, and Present
Interpretive Programs and Services

Where Are We in the Interpretive Planning Process?

Before we get started with this section of our interpretive planning process, let's take a minute to review where we are. We had stated that the WHAT, WHY, and WHO sections of the interpretive plan were done first. Once we have compiled and analyzed the information for each of these sections, and have identified all of the potential interpretive sites within our park, forest, or site, then the next step is to take a look at each interpretive resource (from the Site Inventory forms). We will have to decide on some specifics about how we want to interpret each of these resources. To facilitate this part of the planning process, we will use Story Development forms and a set procedure for doing our detailed resource site planning for our Interpretive Master Plan.

Here's How I Do It

First of all, remember that there are an interpretive theme and objectives for the whole site. The **theme** is the key here; the interpretation at each resource site must focus on illustrating the main interpretive theme.

For each Interpretive Resource Inventory form, I will complete a set of story development forms. Let's take a closer look at each of the forms.

Story Development Form A

On this form, for each interpretive resource inventoried, indicate:

- The Site Index Number of the resource. This helps keep track of all the resources and can be used to locate them on a resource map.
- The resource name.
- The theme for interpreting this resource. Note: The theme should relate to the main site interpretive theme.
- Site objectives. What sorts of development or engineering are needed to prepare the site for visitors? List here objectives such as adding a parking lot, doing rehabilitation work, putting in a boardwalk, etc.
- Interpretive Program and Services Objectives. These are the specific objectives that interpretation is to accomplish at this resource location.

Figures 22a, 22b, and 22c illustrate a blank Planning Form A and then an example of a completed Form A from a past project. Feel free to copy the blank planning form for your own use in interpretive planning.

Story Development Form B

I use this form for indicating the kind(s) of interpretive media or services that could be used at this location. I use a whole page for this form so that, over time, photos (of signs, boardwalks, etc.), draft interpretive label text, notes, copies of design options, etc. can be added. Think of this space as a conceptual flypaper bulletin board. You can "stick" your ideas here. In the beginning, list all potential media or services. Then you can select specific media based on final budgets or other planning realities.

Figures 23a and 23b show a blank Planning Form B and then an example of a completed Form B from a past project. Feel free to copy the blank Form B for your own use.

Story Development Form C

I use this form for backup. The justification section is just that. If you think that someone may balk at your recommendations for development of a given resource, or at your recommended media, this is the place to do your "offensive" planning. Try to anticipate any objections and lay out your rationale here. In addition, the Planners Comments section allows you space to present any other information about this site and how you think it should be interpreted. Depending on the kind of interpretive plan you are doing, you may feel that you do not need to use this form at all, which is OK. These planning forms are TOOLS to help us plan more effectively. Feel free to add to or change any of these forms to better suit your needs.

Figures 24a and 24b show a blank Planning Form C and an example of a completed Form C from a past project. Feel free to copy the blank form for your own planning use.

Story Development – Form A		Page of
Site Index No:	Site Name:	

Interpretive Theme:

Site Objectives:

Interpretive Program Objectives:

Interpretive Concepts –

Figure 22a.

Site Index No: B-5   Site Name: Fire Zone

Interpretive Theme:

The theme for this site should center around the effects of fire on a forest environment.

Site Objectives:

To provide a location where visitors may obtain information about the effects of fire on a forest.

To provide year-round access to this site.

To protect the site by controlling visitor flow through site by means of a trail through the area.

To encourage visitation into this area of Price Nature Center.

Interpretive Program Objectives:

1. A majority of the visitors will gain a basic understanding of the effects of fire on the ecology of a forest.

2. A majority of the visitors will gain a basic understanding of the effects of the fire on Price Nature Center.

3. A majority of the visitors will gain a understanding of fire safety/prevention methods they should use to prevent such fires.

Note: These are very general objectives which could be made more specific once actual programs were planned.

Interpretive Concepts:

A variety of concepts could be interpreted at this site very effectively. A brief list for consideration is provided on the following page.

Figure 22b.

Interpretive Concepts -

1. Both the beneficial and harmful effects of a forest fire
   could be interpreted, such as the use of fire in habitat
   management vs. uncontrolled fire.

2. The use of fire in a forest from a historical viewpoint.
   For example, forest fires were sometimes ignited by North
   American Indians to clear the woods of undergrowth,
   facilitating travel and improving visibility for hunting
   and creating grassy openings for deer.

3. There are three basic forms of fires: 1) Ground fire - which
   consumes organic material beneath the forest floor. Slow
   moving, hard to suppress fires in peat beds or bogs are
   typical of this form. 2) Surface fire - the fire burns leaves,
   twigs and other fuels on the forest floor. The fire at Price
   Nature Center in 1966 was a surface fire. 3) Crown fire -
   this is a fire that burns through the tops of the trees,
   consuming fuels from the ground up to the top of the forest
   canopy.

4. The concepts of fire safety and prevention could be
   interpreted such as being careful with campfires, etc.

These are a few suggestions for main concepts to be interpreted
in this site. For more information on interpreting forest
fires, please see the publication "Forest Interpreter's Primer
on Fire Management". This publication is available free from
the U.S. Forest Service, Washington, D.C.

Figure 22c.

Story Development – Form B		Page of

Site Index No:	Site Name:

Interpretive Mode(s):

Figure 23a.

| Site Index No: B-5 | Site Name: Fire Zone |

Interpretive Mode(s):

A variety of interpretive modes could be utilized for interpreting this story to the public. These include:

1. Interpretor conducted programs/guided hikes in this site.

2. The use of interpretive signs at selected locations interpreting the effects of fire, fire ecology, effects of fire on wildlife and plants, fire safety/prevention, or other related topics.

3. The use of an interpretive publication which could address several topics related to the effects of fire on the forest environment.

4. An interpretive exhibit at the interpretive (nature) center.

Figure 23b.

Story Development – Form C		Page of

Site Index No:	Site Name:

Justification:

Planner's Comments:

Figure 24a.

Site Index No: B-5   Site Name: Fire Zone

Justification:

This site is fairly unique in the Saginaw area in that it is the only site in the area where fire interpretation could be offered at an actual fire site. Also, the effects of fire on the ecology of a forest (and Price Nature Center) is an important aspect of an overall interpretation of Price Nature Center and the ecology of the area.

Interpretive signs could be placed at key locations along the trail planned for this site to provide year round interpretation of this theme.

The use of interpretive brochures may be the most effective means of interpretation here until such time as a interpretor is available to offer programs on the fire theme. Brochures could be produced "in house" and could cover more details than could be interpreted with a sign. Brochures can also be taken home with visitors and have added educational use in this respect.

Planner's Comments:

As this is a fairly unique site in Price Nature Center, the interpretation of fires effects on a forest should not be over-looked. A copy of the brief report on the forest fire which occurred in October, 1966 at Price Forest is provided for reference as Appendix D to this plan.

Figure 24b.

The Planning Form Set

In the interpretive plan document (I use a three-ring notebook so that the plan can be easily updated or corrected as needed), I put the Site Inventory Form for each interpretive resource and the three Story Development Forms together as one set. This set for each interpretive resource becomes, in fact, a mini site development plan for each interpretive resource site. The combined set of these planning forms, one set for each resource inventoried, becomes the guts of the interpretive master plan for the whole site. They tell exactly what resource sites within the park or forest need to be developed, why, and which media or interpretive services to use.

Use of the planning forms is not intended to limit the creativity of interpretive planners, but merely to provide a place to write their creative ideas down so the ideas can be fulfilled.

Figures 25a-c are an example of a complete planning form set developed for one interpretive resource site from a past project.

Summary

This series of interpretive planning forms was designed to make interpretive plans easier to prepare, understand, implement, and update. Having a standardized set of forms (whether you use these or design your own) for interpretive resource site inventory and story development will help to ensure that all the desired types of information an interpretive plan should contain are included in the Master Plan.

The use of standardized interpretive planning forms can aid in the development of interpretive systems plans (discussed later in this book) for parks, forests, historic sites, or related tourism sites within a geographical region or state or county park system.

These forms are tools that I have developed and used during many years of field testing, so I know that they work for me. But I am always looking for ways to improve them. Use them if you like, or develop your own format. But the forms approach will save you time and ensure accuracy and uniformity during the whole planning process.

Interpretive Site Inventory

Site Index #: H-1

Site Name: Carp River Forge Site

Site Location:

See attached site index map.

Site Description:

This site is composed of several industrial/archaeological features including:
1) water wheel & mill race; 2) causeway; 3) dam; 4) furnace sites; 5) slag pile,
and 6) remains of the mill pond.

Seasonal Accessibility:

Access to this site is closed until future development and archaeological studies
have been completed. Future access will be via trail and board walk with
viewing platforms of the various features.

Interpretive Significance:

This is the major interpretive resource complex of the Michigan Iron Industry
Museum site, and represents the location of the first iron manufactory in the Lake Supe-
rior Region. A copy of the 1973 archaeological report on this site appears as Appendix A,
and a copy of the 1974 archaeological report appears as Appendix B in the Interpretive
Plan.

Photos and graphics appear on the
following pages.

Attach Photo Here

Figure 25a.

Story Development
Form A

Site Index #: H-1

Site Name: Carp River Forge Site

Interpretive Theme:

This was the birth site of the Michigan Iron Industry.

Site Development Objectives

- To restrict access to this site until such time as all archaeological work on the site has been completed.

- To provide visitor interpretation and limited visitor access to this site once archaeological surveys have been completed.

- To develop some limited reconstruction of building locations on the site by providing outlines of building locations with location keys (building and function).

Interpretive Program Objectives:

- The majority of the visitors will learn that this site was the birth place of the Michigan Iron Industry.

- The majority of the visitors will gain a general overview of the history timeline of this site.

- The majority of the visitors will be able to imagine what it must have been like to have been some of the early workers here (hardships, etc.).

- The majority of the visitors will understand how the iron was forged from the iron ore.

- All visitors will understand the need to help protect this site, and stay on the boardwalk.

- The majority of the visitors will want to go to the visitor center to see and learn more about the iron industry that once operated here.

Figure 25b.

Story Development
Form B

Site Index #: H-1

Site Name: Carp River Forge Site

Interpretive Services or Media Recommendations:

The main mode for interpreting the forge site is currently from a viewing area (F-3 on the site index map). It is suggested that a new viewing area with observation platform be constructed (F-1 on the site index map) to provide a better overview of the site resources. Interpretive panels would be utilized to illustrate the site from a historical reconstruction viewpoint, as well as to interpret the daily activities that once went on here.

Later on, a complete boardwalk loop trail can be designed to guide visitors over and around the complete site, with interpretive panels, or self-guiding brochure interpreting each specific feature.

The boardwalk would allow access to this site for all visitors, including those in wheelchairs.

Estimated cost for interpretive panels (using fiberglass embedment) would be $2,000 per panel.

Estimated cost for the boardwalk would be $25 per linear foot (based on the latest cost estimate from potential contractors).

Estimated cost for self-guiding trail brochure for the boardwalk would be $1,200 for one 8 1/2 x 11" (two fold) brochure - photo ready.

Figure 25c.

I&O: Implementation and Operations

Making it Happen!

The main purpose of the Implementation & Operations Section is to provide in one place the total implementation phasing and costs for the interpretive plan. Realize that you will probably not be able to implement ALL of the interpretive plan at one time. And it may be difficult to accurately predict future costs and resource needs. To simplify this process, you may want to **phase** the development over time. Five years works well as an average period for implementing the total interpretive plan.

The I&O Implementation Matrix

The matrix format is the easiest way to present the implementation needs for the entire plan. Figures 26a and 26b, on the following pages, show one matrix format that I use.

Obtain the site index number from each interpretive planning form set. The list of services or media also comes from the planning forms. Some of the items will come from the "site objectives" part of Form A (develop a new boardwalk, for example). Others will come from the Media section (Form B), such as "develop a new wayside exhibit panel for this site."

The fiscal year that you want to "implement" that particular part of the plan is up to you, but I suggest that you make your check marks in pencil. The cost estimates come from your in-house staff and contractors.

In addition to the implementation of the "hardware" of the plan, you may also want to do a similar kind of matrix for recommended staffing needs. Figure 27 illustrates a staffing operations need, again from a past project.

Summary

The I&O section of the interpretive plan is your strategy for how you want to implement the plan. It includes an analysis of all the site development, media development, and (if appropriate) future staffing needs. Try to make sure that your list of budget items is complete, and that your cost estimates are the best you can get (they should be fairly representative and accurate).

Use a pencil to plan your development priorities (phasing) for each of the items; you never know how your budget may change.

Interpretive Services Needs Assessment

Site Index #

Interpretive Media & Services

FY Implementation
93 94 95 96 97

Cost Estimates

Figure 26a.

Interpretive Services Needs Assessment

Site Index #	Interpretive Media & Services	93	94	95	96	97	98	99	20	01	02	Cost Estimates
KR-1	Trailhead sign for the Lost Coast Trail			x								$3800. (incl. mountings)
KR-2	Interp. Viewing Area Platform for estuary.					x						$7000.00
	Interpretive Panels (2) 2X3'					x						$2500 each
	Develop Interp. brochure on estuary (photo ready)					x						$1500.00
	Develop teachers packet on estuary ecology							x				$3000.00 (in house)
KR-3	Interpretive panels (2x3')							x				$2500 each
KR-4	Interpretive panel (2x3')				x							$2500.00
KR-5	Develop pull-off area.		x									$1000.00
	Interpretive panel (2x3')		x									$2500.00

Figure 26b.

Agency: Metro Parks
Park/Site: Blacklick Woods   Page __/__ of __/__

Position   Target Date

	/ 1985 /	1986 /	1987 /	1988 /	1989 /
Naturalist III				2080	2080
Naturalist II	2080	2080	2080		2080
Naturalist I	2080	2080	2080	2080	2080
Naturalist I		*PT 9mo Seaso-nal. 10hrwk 360	*PT 9mo @10hr wk 360	PT 9mo 15hr wk 540	
Naturalist Intern	Sp/Su 1040	6 mo @40hr 1040	6mo @ 40hr 1040	6mo @ 40hr wk 1040	6mo @ 40 hr wk 1040
	5200	5560	5560	5740	7280

*Some programming at Pickerington Ponds

Figure 27.

The SO WHAT Section

The So WHAT Section of the interpretive plan provides direction for evaluation of the recommended, new, or existing interpretive programs and services. It provides answers to the question, "How will I know if my objectives have been accomplished?"

In order to maintain high quality interpretation, it is essential to be able to critically appraise the effectiveness of the interpretive programs and services offered to visitors. The crucial questions to be asked and answered are (from Veverka, 1977):

1. Are the objectives of the total interpretive program (whole site, park, forest, zoo, facility) being met at an acceptable level?
2. Are the objectives of individual interpretive sites (from the site inventory and story development forms) being met at an acceptable level?

But what does the term "acceptable level" mean? If your objective stated that "the majority of the visitors will...", that means your acceptable level is at least 51 percent accomplishment. But if you wanted at least 60 percent of the visitors to....., then your acceptable level is at least 60 percent. You determine what is acceptable for you when you write the objective.

Plan Evaluation into Your Project

The evaluation section should recommend evaluation as part of the planning and design process for any new or recommended interpretive program or service, or any interpretive site development. For example, you could have a statement in this section recommending that all interpretive text for signs, exhibits, brochures, and so on be pre-tested before actually being produced. You might recommend an evaluation strategy for your agency for pre-testing or doing formative evaluation for new exhibits or services. You might also recommend yearly visitor services evaluations ("are visitors understanding the site theme? Are site interpretive objectives being accomplished?").

The Evaluation Process

The six main parts of the evaluation process are:

1. Identify the objectives that you want to evaluate.
2. Select the most appropriate evaluation technique or tool.
3. Apply the technique and obtain results. A time table on when and how you are going to do the evaluation(s) can be a helpful tool.
4. Compare actual results to the results desired from the objective.
5. Do an analysis of the results (Did you accomplish your objectives? Why or why not?).
6. Make recommendations for improvement.

Some Evaluation Techniques

There are a lot of ways to do evaluation depending on the program or service, agency rules about surveying visitors directly, and other circumstances. The following matrix (Table 1) presents some of the more common evaluation techniques, a brief description of the technique, and pros or cons about each.

Suggested Reading List on Evaluation

There is a lot to learn about why, how, and when to evaluate interpretive programs and services. Here is a list of suggested readings on evaluation to help you in this area.

Ham, Sam H. 1986. "Social Program Evaluation and Interpretation: A Literature Review" in Machlis, Gary E. (ed.) *Interpretive Views*. National Parks and Conservation Association.

Lewis, William. 1980. *Interpreting for Park Visitors*. Philadelphia, PA: Eastern National Park and Monument Association.

Medlin, Nancy C. and Sam H. Ham. 1992. *A Handbook For Evaluating Interpretive Services*. Prepared for the USDA Forest Service, Intermountain Region.

Medlin, N.C. and Machlis, G.E. 1991. *Focus Groups: A Tool For Evaluating Interpretive Services*. Moscow, ID: Cooperative Park Studies Unit, College of Forestry, Wildlife, and Range Sciences, University of Idaho.

Tabb, George E. (ed.). 1990. *Report of Findings: NAI/Federal Interagency Council Workshop on Evaluating the Effectiveness of Interpretation*. Madison, WI.

Table 1 Evaluative Techniques for Interpretive Services (after Wagar, 1976; Veverka, et al, 1977)

Evaluative Technique	Description	Pros	Cons	Comments
Direct Audience Feedback	Interpretor analyzes visitors' responses in face-to-face settings	Allows for immediate analysis of visitor's reaction to the interpretor and service. The interpretor can change his/her approach on the spot to elicit a better response from the visitors.	Technique is subjective since the interpetor must "interpret" the visitor's reaction to him/herself and the service.	The number of questions visitors ask, facial expressions, restlessness, etc. are often good indicators of enjoyment, boredom, etc.
Auditing By An Expert	Have an experienced interpretor watch and critique an interpretive presentation.	Allows for the input of more experience professionals into interpretive programming.	The expert judges how s/he thinks a presentation will affect a visitor. Thus, subjective.	In the case where live presentations cannot be evaluated on site, video tapes can be used.
Direct Measures of Behavior	Determine what interpretive service options visitors take when given a choice (i.e. hike vs. movie)	Allows for the determination of which services are most preferred.	Can determine what services visitors prefer but not why.	This type of information usually determined by head counts, ticket stubs etc. The technique could be used in conjunction with a questionaire or interview to determine why visitors made certain choices.
Observation of Audience Attention	Plant scanners in audience to watch and document how many people are focusing their eyes on the interpretor.	Allows for the determination of visitor responses during a presentation.	Assumes that watching the interpretor is synonymous with interest, understanding, enjoyment, etc.	

Table I.

Table 1 Continued

Evaluative Technique	Description	Pros	Cons	Comments
Length of Viewing or Listening Time	Compare the amount of time people look at or listen to a presentation with the amount of time it would take to completely read or hear it.	Allows for the determination of whether or not people are spending enough time with an exhibit, sign, etc. to absorb the entire message.	Cannot determine visitor enjoyment, understanding, or interest. Thus, no judgment can be made as to whether or not the message is too long.	Shiner and Shafer found that "visitors looked at displays only 15 to 64 percent of the total time required to read or listen to the total message presented." " ... the longer the printed or recorded message...the shorter the viewing time"
Questionnaire	A written set of questions given to visitors to determine demographic and experiencial data.	A great deal of visitor information can be obtained with a well-designed questionnaire. Questions concerning specific services can be incorporated into the questionnaire.	Subject to written response bias. Time-consuming to design, administer and evaluate.	A major problem with many questionnaires is that they are designed and written to elicit the responses the researcher wants. Great care must be taken to design a questionnaire as objectively as possible.
Interviews	Similar to questionnaires except that questions are administered orally.	Same advanatges as questionnaires. Often a preferred method of data collection since "many people are more willing to communicate orally than in writing"	Similar problems as with questionnaires in terms of designing objective questions	

Table I(cont).

Table 1 Continued

Evaluative Techniques	Description	Pros	Cons	Comments
Self-Testing Devices	Mechanical devices operated by the visitor to answer questions or uncover more interpretive information.	Allows for active participation of visitors. A "fun" technique of evaluation from the visitor's point of view.	Subject to mechanical breakdowns and vandalism. Often monopolized by children.	For further reference see Wagar (1972).
Panel of Outsiders	A panel of people not associated with interpretation nor the subject matter being presented are asked to evaluate a service.	The panel can point out the strengths and weaknesses of a service before it is ever presented to the public.	The evaluation will only be as objective as the panel members chosen.	
Other Unobtrusive Measures*	Look at fingerprints and noseprints on glass, footwear, litter (such as leaflets, cigarette butts, etc.). Look at products of depreciative behavior (graffiti, vandalism, etc.)	May indicate heavy use or a basic design problem.	Do not know <u>why</u> areas are being used so extensively nor the specific design flow.	This information often-times can be gleaned by talking to maintenance personnel.
Suggestion Box	A locked box where visitors can drop any comments or suggestions.	Anonymity.	Usually get comments biased towards a positive or negative extreme.	In relation to Malabar, the box should be located in VIC as a general catch-a for comments concerning all services.

*These catagories have been added by the authors and three of Wagar's original categories were deleted.
(from Malabar Farm: An Interpretive Planning Process, Veverka, Willis, et al, 1977)

Table I(cont).

Chapter Three The Interpretive Planning Process

Interpretive
Systems Planning

Working Cooperatively

When we try to pick out anything by itself,
we find it hitched to everything else in the Universe.
- John Muir

This quotation from John Muir points out one of the challenges for interpretive planning today. While interpretive master planning is generally regarded as essential to the success of any interpretive site or facility, the majority of such plans are site, facility, or park specific, with little attention to a regional context and integration with interpretation at other nearby sites or facilities. Agencies with interpretive planning responsibilities covering extensive areas generally emphasize only those facets or stories directly pertaining to and within the scope of their concern. Little attention is paid to the interface between an agency's mandate and the private sector regarding interpretive stories, themes, and facilities. As a result, a large percentage of interpretive efforts tend to be rather narrow in their potential to market regional stories and interpretive opportunities.

What is a Systems Approach?

The systems approach is simply a way of looking at the entire system of interpretive agencies, sites, facilities, and opportunities around you or in your region. There are many different kinds of "systems" that you can plan for:

- A regional park district might have three, four, or more parks managed by one agency. Systems planning would look at developing an interpretive plan for the whole system of parks, seeking the common theme or story that the whole system illustrates.
- A state park system would look at planning for all of the parks as one unit, with interpretive objectives, etc. for the whole state.

- A regional interpretive system plan could be a tourism plan as well. In this kind of planning, different interpretive opportunities available within a given geographical region are analyzed for interrelated themes and interpretive opportunities. This may include a national forest, a nearby state or county park, a local historical museum or historic site, a local zoo, etc. The interpretive systems plan would look at how these sites could share stories, opportunities, and visitors—not competing but rather complementing each other.

As an example of how interpretive systems planning might work, let's say that three parks are administered by a given agency, Park A, Park B, and Park C. Due to the historic resources and features each park contains, the interpretive planners decide that these parks would be most effective for the interpretation of the state's history from prehistoric times to the present. Figure 28 illustrates how, with an interpretive systems approach, these parks can interface with each other.

Park A may be best suited for interpreting state history from early Indian times to the 1800s. Park B may have the best resources for interpreting the state history from 1800 to 1890. Park C may be the best to interpret the state's history from 1890 to present.

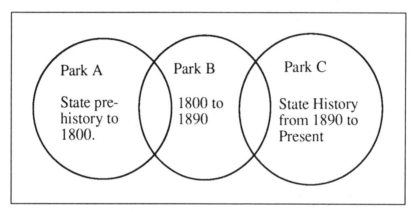

Figure 28.

In this simplified example, using the systems approach to interpretive planning, each of the three parks within the same administrative system contributes a unique and complementary facet to the major theme of "The State Parks offer a unique setting to experience our State's dramatic history," or other related theme.

The systems approach helps to focus each park on interpreting the specific story that it is best able to illustrate, while not competing with or unnecessarily duplicating stories told at other parks. Note that it is OK to overlap some of the story presentation from park to park. While, in this example, the contribution of Native American history may be found at all three parks, each park could interpret a different aspect of the Native American story, with the main presentation being at Park A. As a result, the interpretation at any one park would not unnecessarily duplicate that at any other, but together they would promote a much bigger story than could be told and illustrated at any one park alone.

A Regional Approach with Different Agencies

The same philosophy works for regional planning with different agencies involved. For example, a national forest may have a strong story to interpret about early logging history and subsequent settlement of the nearby town. A local museum may have the actual artifacts and historical documents associated with the early logging history and settlement. A state park may have a good example of a homestead site from that settlement period. A commercial tour company may give guided bus tours through the region to these, and other related historic and cultural sites. If they plan to work and interpret together, each can enjoy a more cost-effective planning effort.

They can also jointly advertise programs and services and develop a regional Heritage Tourism or Ecotourism program. They can "share" markets rather than compete for parts of markets.

The Value of the Systems Approach

- It integrates related facilities, themes, and stories within an agency or with several agencies.
- It facilitates a variety of levels of experience or "interpretive pacing" for visitor with a common thread of experience on a regional or system-wide level.
- It facilitates the use of natural, historical, and cultural resources that might otherwise be ignored or overlooked.
- It enhances optimal use of available physical, financial, and psychological resources within an area or region.
- It encourages a more expedient and rational approach to planning interpretive services along historic corridors or scenic byways, which may access areas or interpretive resources of many different agencies and communities.
- It is the main tool for developing heritage tourism plans, for determining the critical mass of tourism opportunities from which to market a region.

Preparing an Interpretive Systems Plan

Preparing an interpretive systems plan can involve both long-range and immediate planning needs. It is probably best to take that proverbial "first step" in developing a systems plan at a smaller scale for immediate needs and letting your interpretive systems plan evolve into your long-range marketing and interpretation plan.

How do you actually develop an interpretive systems plan? There are five criteria that should be considered when developing your plan:

1. Relative levels of a resource story's significance and its attraction and appeal to visitors for all sites and facilities.
2. Willingness of different agencies, sites, and facilities to work together.

3. Needed availability of the resource or story relative to visitor demand and interest within the region or system.
4. Potential of a site or story to enhance the intrinsic variety of all themes within the system, contrasted to merely adding more of what already exists within the system.
5. Potential for building cooperative partnerships for cost sharing and developing win-win relationships. Remember, for a partnership to be successful, both partners need to benefit from the relationship.

The System Planning Process

The interpretive planning process for a whole system is the same as that used for developing an interpretive plan for one park or site. That means you need to consider and plan for:

WHAT

Do a survey of key existing resources and interpretive opportunities for each of the different sites or facilities that will be part of the regional or agency system. Based on the resources that a given park or site has, develop an appropriate main interpretive theme for that site—just as you would for developing an interpretive master plan. This is where you decide what parts of what theme each site will be responsible for, and how much, if any, duplication of story line will be needed. For example, if a local museum only has a small portion of its exhibits on logging history, it may play a smaller role in the systems plan presentation of that theme.

Figure 29 illustrates how the main interpretive theme from four different sites (park, historic site, national forest, and museum for example) could be linked to illustrate one "Big Picture" interpretive theme for a region or community.

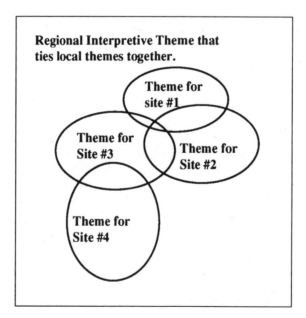

Figure 29.

Can you always find one main interpretive theme? Probably—and it may be very broad and general. But in developing the main theme for the system or region, use the same approach as developing your main interpretive theme for a park, historic site, zoo, or other facility. Ask yourself (and the planning team) the question, "If a visitor visits all of the parks within the agency system—or all of the sites within a regional system—if they only remember one thing about our system, or the regional story, what do we want that one thing to be?" The answer will be your theme.

But if your regional story is too big and you feel that you need to have two or three different main themes, the interpretive police won't come and arrest you. It's OK to have more than one main theme...it is just harder to market. When at all possible, I recommend having only one main theme.

WHY

Develop your specific interpretive objectives for the whole system, and then for each individual park or interpretive site or facility. For example:

- The majority of visitors to the town of Smithville will learn about other nearby interpretive attractions to visit.
- The majority of visitors will be encouraged to visit other attractions, via self-guiding or guided tours.
- The majority of visitors will feel the sense of "regional pride" the people and businesses of this community have for its local heritage.
- The majority of visitors will understand how the logging industry affected the town of Smithville, and nearby communities, in the 1890s.

WHO

Do a market analysis of existing and potential visitorship within the region. What markets do all of the sites within the system have in common, and which markets are unique to them? Who are your visitors? When are they visiting? Why are they visiting? How long is their average visit? You will need to look at visitor-use patterns for each park and site within the system as well.

HOW/WHEN/WHERE

Look at how, when, and where interpretive programs and services can be offered. This is your specific analysis of program potential and your strategy for presenting the themes to the visitors. This follows the HOW/WHEN/WHERE approach used for park or site interpretive master plans, and you can use the same Story Development forms.

But in addition, you will need to analyze the movement of visitors to and through the region, and to each of the sites within the system. For example, will you try to develop a scenic byway or auto tour to each site? Will the programs and services of each site be advertised at the partner sites?

Implementation and Operations

This section details how you intend to get the systems plan into action. What will be needed? What will it cost? Who will do it?

Probably the easiest way to view an interpretive systems plan is as a collection of interpretive plans from different parks and sites within the system (Figure 30), or from different sites and facilities within a region, connected by a common story or "big picture" to be shared and presented to all visitors.

For example, the main interpretive theme for the tourism system illustrated in Figure 30 might be "The affect of the historic logging industry in Carlton County can best be seen and experienced in and around the community of Smithville." Each site or facility would contribute to illustrating or supporting that story, even though it may not be *their* main story.

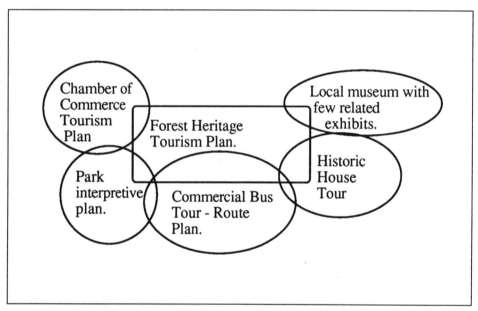

Figure 30.

Remember, real success in tourism (and interpretation) efforts in the 1990s and beyond will require a new way of thinking about what, why, and how we offer interpretive opportunities to visitors. Our individual parks, forests, cultural and historic sites, and zoos do not exist in a vacuum, but are part of a regional system already. The question is then not one of, "do you want your site or facility to be part of the system?", but rather a question of, "how successful do you want your site or facility to be?" considering it already exists within a system, even though the relationships between different sites and facilities may not be formalized.

In general, doing system-wide or regional interpretive planning is necessary if you plan to tie into existing or potential tourism opportunities. Use the interpretive systems plan as a marketing plan. Interpretive systems planning is just good business.

Chapter Summary

In this chapter we looked at the interpretive planning process as a whole, and saw examples of how all of the planning sections would be put together to develop an interpretive plan for a whole site. As illustrated on the interpretive plan outline, each section of the planning process would also be a section on the interpretive plan. The main bulk of the interpretive master plan for a given park, forest, historic site, or other unit, would be made up of the planning forms for each individual interpretive resource within the site. The planning forms and planning approach I use are tools that work for me. Based on many years of field testing, they produce very complete and accessible planning documents. We have also seen the need to think and plan for a regional or system-wide approach to make planning more effective and to avoid duplication of efforts.

In the following chapters we will take a closer look at how you can use this same planning process for planning other kinds of interpretive services, such as trails and exhibits.

References

Cherem, G.J. 1977. "The professional interpretor: agent for an awakening giant." *Association of Interpretive Naturalists Journal*. Vol. 2(1)

Cordell, H., G. James and R. Griffith. 1970. "Estimating recreation use at visitor information centers." USDA Forest Service Research Paper SE-69. November.

Elvidge, J.A. 1991. "The Interpretive Desires of Overnight Visitors at Four Campgrounds in Coulee Dam National Recreation Area." M.S. Thesis, University of Washington.

Ham, S.H. 1992. *Environmental Interpretation: A Practical Guide for People with Big Ideas and Small Budgets*. Golden, Co: North American Press.

Lewis, W.J. 1980. *Interpreting for Park Visitors*. Philadelphia, PA: Eastern National Park and Monument Association.

Maslow, A.H. 1954. *Motivation and Personality*. Harper & Row, New York.

National Park Service Technical Services Division, Western Region. "Marketing Parks and Recreation." Venture Publishing, Inc. (No date).

Veverka, J.A. 1978. "A Survey and Analysis of Park Visitor Motivations for Selecting and Attending Interpretive Programs." M.S. Thesis, The Ohio State University School of Natural Resources, Columbus, Ohio.

Veverka, J.A. 1978. "Pacing interpretive services: a concept for interpretive planners." *Journal of Interpretation*, Vol. III, No. 1.

Veverka, J.A. 1979. "A systems approach to interpretive planning." *Journal of Interpretation*, Vol. IV, No. 1.

Veverka, J.A. 1990. *Interpretive Master Planning*. John Veverka & Associates Training Division, Course manual.

Veverka, J.A. 1991. "Developing interpretive master plans." In *Proceedings, Heritage Interpretation International Third Global Congress*. Nov. 3-8, 1991.

Veverka, J.A. 1992. *An Objective Look at Interpretation*. John Veverka & Associates. Occasional Paper, Interpretive Training Division. March.

Wagar, A.J., G. Lovelady and H. Falkin. 1976. "Evaluation techniques for interpretation: study results from an exhibition on energy." USDA Forest Service Research Paper PNW-221.

White, R.W. 1959. "Motivation reconsidered: The concept of competence." In *Psychological Review*. 66, 313-324.

Chapter Four

Planning and Designing Interpretive Self-guiding Trails, Tours, and Byways

The art of becoming wise is the art of knowing what to overlook.
- William James, Psychologist

Planning Self-guiding Trails

For most parks, forests, nature centers, botanical gardens, and other outdoor sites, the self-guiding trail is often one of the most used of all interpretive services. This is particularly true if the agency has limited staff for conducted programs or a visitation pattern that would not allow enough people on-site at one time to have a guided trail walk.

The process used to actually plan and design a self-guiding trail (SGT) can vary widely from planner to planner, depending on the planner's experience with trails. The process outlined here is the one I use most of the time because I know from experience that it works. But planners should feel free to modify this process based on their own desires and the specific demands of the trail project they are working on.

The New SGT

Let's begin with the process I use for planning a brand new SGT. Assume for this example that the trail will be in a national forest. At the start of the planning process bear in mind that this new SGT must illustrate the main interpretive theme or story line of the forest (or ranger district). An SGT is a tool—a way to provide an example or to help illustrate the main interpretive theme (refer back to Figure 6 on page 26).

But what do you do if there is no interpretive plan or main theme for the forest (as is often the case)? Create one! Do a quick assessment of the resources of the forest, discuss potential themes with Forest Service staff, and develop a Main Interpretive Theme. Although this theme may change over time, it lends focus while planning for the content and location of the trail.

Even before the more formal process of SGT planning begins, you should be thinking of the best location options for where to put the SGT. Given the typically large land area that most national forests have, this could be a quite a task. Over the years I have developed Veverka's Law Number 1 for SGT planning: "Put the SGT as close to where the visitors are as possible!" This means that the FIRST places I begin to consider for locations for a new SGT are within walking distance from the most heavily used campgrounds. Here are the reasons for this decision.

- Many visitors arrive with campers or other rigs. Once they settle into a campsite, they don't want to have to drive anywhere.
- To make the trail and its media cost effective, you want as many people as possible to use the trail.
- You can use the trail as a marketing tool to make visitors aware of other interpretive programs and services in other parts of the park or forest.
- Visitors will be more likely to use an SGT that is nearby and takes a short time to walk.

I know from experience that SGTs that are close to campgrounds will get frequent use. One trail we planned near a campground at Lassen National Forest on the Eagle Lake District has the same visitors walking the trail almost daily because it is nearby, scenic, and an easy half-hour walk.

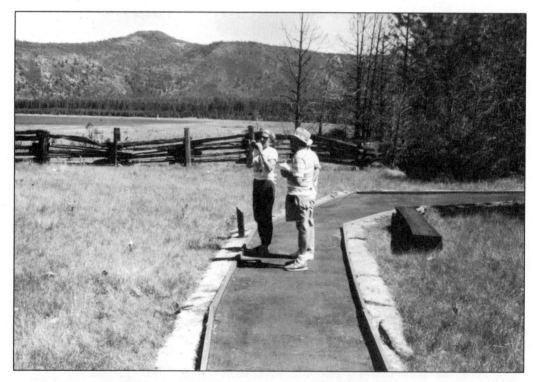

Hidden Change Interpretive Trail, Lassen National Forest, California. Being located close to a campground, the trail received a lot of daily use.

The Planning Process

The planning process we use for new trails follows the same format as developing interpretive plans.

WHAT

- Determine the most appropriate location for the SGT, such as near a campground (Figure 31).

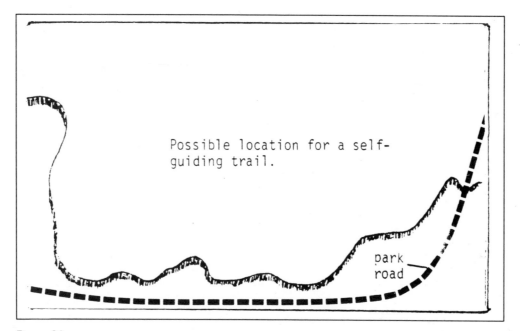

Figure 31.

- Next, walk the area to thoroughly inventory all of its major interpretive resources. It helps to make a photocopy enlargement of a topo map of the area, and note the location of each resource on the map.
- After assessing all of the major interpretive resources within the trail area, scan your notes to see if a theme jumps out at you. What does the site best illustrate? What is its story? (Figure 32).

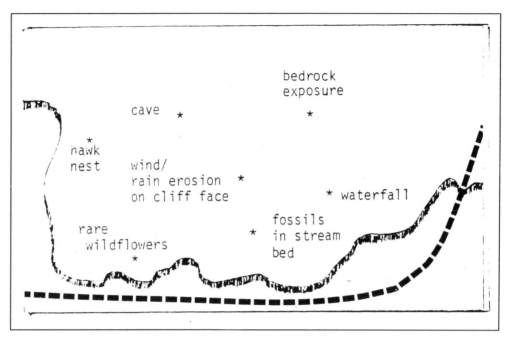

Figure 32.

■ From this analysis it appears that geology is the strongest topic for this
area. To layout the trail, draw a line connecting the dots at each of the
geological resource sites (Figure 33). In this way, the trail will lead the
visitor to each resource that is part of a definite story.

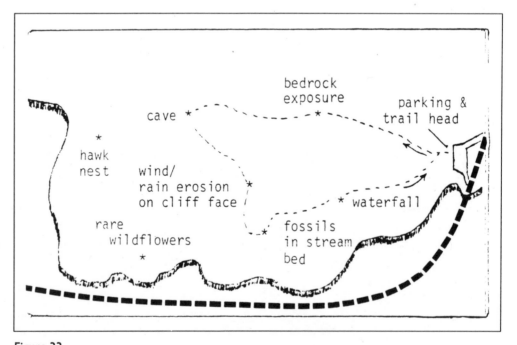

Figure 33.

Note: When you are ready for this step of "connecting the dots," you need to walk the proposed route to consider:

- The most pleasing visual route (bends in the trail) to actually connect the stops.
- Look for potentenial physical problems with your route (exposed tree roots or rock outcrops on the trail your visitor might trip on).
- Look for any possible maintenance problems, such as areas that are wet, or stay wet after a rain. Building board walks, or putting in trail drainage systems for wet areas is more expensive than simply going around them.
- Will the slope of the trail (if any) be too steep for visitors, will the trail be used by visitors in wheelchairs?
- If trail needs to go up slope, once the trail is cut, will there be any potential erosion problems? Will you need to put in water run-off bars?
- Will you need to construct any steps or handrails? What would that cost?

I suggest that if you need extra help with trail maintenance or physical design issues, consult one of the trail design reference books listed in the reference section of this chapter for more ideas on maintenance/design considerations. Be sure to check with your "in house" landscape architect or maintenance staff as well.

- Based on the resources, develop one main interpretive theme for the trail. In this case, for example, the theme might be, "The rocks of the Smith Forest hold many secrets." Remember that each stop on the SGT should illustrate this theme.

WHY

As part of the planning process you must also develop specific objectives that the SGT is to accomplish. This includes learning, behavioral, and emotional objectives. Once you have the inventory and theme, you can develop the objectives. Here are some possible objectives for the Smith Forest SGT:

- The majority of visitors will be able to see first hand how the geology of the area reveals something of its long-ago (and recent) history. *Learn and Do*
- The majority of visitors will be able to find or see fossils in the stream bed. *Do*
- The majority of visitors will understand how wind and rain affect the landscape. *Learn*
- The majority of visitors will be amazed to learn that the geology of this area affects the kinds of plants and animals that can live here. *Emotional*
- The majority of visitors will want to learn more about the geology of the region and attend one of the summer geology programs. *Learn and Do*
- All visitors will treat this resource in a safe manner and with a sense of respect and stewardship. *Emotional and Do*
- The majority of visitors will understand and remember the theme of the trail. *Learn*

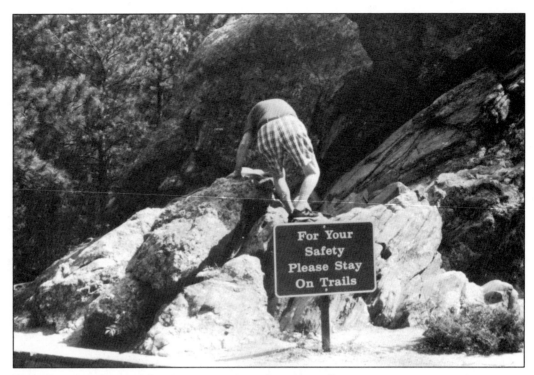

The behavioral objectives for this sign aren't working too well.

These objectives provide the planner with guidelines for the content of each trail stop presentation. These guidelines can be added to or changed at any time, but by having objectives, the planner can evaluate each step of the process to see if the objectives are being met. The objectives also help in developing interpretive graphics and text for each stop on the trail.

WHO

Another consideration in trail planning and design is who the intended audience will be. For example, if the trail is near a campground, and you know that the campground has a lot of older visitors, the trail should take that into account by having benches and rest stops at suitable intervals. If the trail will be used by a lot of formal school groups, the design should probably have wider paths, with space for groups to meet around each stop or station. Also take into account safety and barrier-free access for visitors with disabilities. Local universities and regional organizations often have staff with expertise on barrier-free trails and other recreational activities.

The analysis of existing or potential visitor use for the trail can also give you some indication as to the kind of interpretive media that may be the most cost effective for the trail. For example, if your trail will have thousands of visitors a year using it, the cost for giving each visitor a self-guiding brochure for the trail might be higher than developing signs-in-place for the trail (a lower cost per visitor contact). But if the trail will serve only a few hundred visitors a year, the cost per visitor contact will be less with brochures.

HOW/WHEN/WHERE

The **HOW** part of planning is to determine how you want to interpret the trail. What kind of media do you want to use? There are many considerations in making this decision. The following chart (Figure 34) provides some comparisons to help you decide which type of trail media to use (modified from Sharpe, 1976).

	Leaflet and Marker	Sign-in-place	Audio (talking label)	Audio (portable cassette)
Initial cost	1	3	4	3
Vandalism	2	4	3	1
Subject to weather	3	2	3	1
Litter potential	4	1	1	1
Potential site for deterioration	2	4	4	1
Aesthetic intrusion	1	3	4	1
Souvenir value of the media	1	4	4	2
Maintenance problems	1	2	4	3
Illustrates progress	3	1	2	4
Easily modified	1	3	2	3
Stocking	4	1	1	1
Distribution of the media	1	1	1	4
Availability sunup to sundown	2	1	1	4
Attention span of the visitor	2	2	1	1
Self-pacing factors	1	1	4	3
Other				
	29	33	37	33

Interpretive Trail Options

Best ← → Worst

1   2   3   4

Figure 34.

I generally give this same advice to any of my clients for whom I do interpretive trail planning. It's Veverka's Law Number 2: "Always do the self-guided trail brochure first." My reason for this is that you can do a very nice SGT brochure on a computer with text, photos, and art work very quickly. This gives you a cost-effective method of pre-testing the content of the brochure. I do a mock-up brochure and give it to a fifth grade class to "critique" for me (I'll talk more about this in the Evaluation section). Then I can make changes, produce a few revised copies, and test these. Within a short time, I will have the brochure "fine tuned" and working at a 80 percent or better effectiveness (my objectives are being accomplished). Consider this. If you were to have a photo-ready brochure done for your trail (contracted out) it would cost you about $1,500 or so. ONE interpretive sign in place can cost this much, or more. Its best to have all of the trail content working and evaluated, then when you know the interpretation works make the signs-in-place. The text or graphics don't change...just the medium they are printed on.

Another consideration for selecting the long-term media for any trail is "What is the media cost per visitor contact over time?" If only 200 visitors a year walk a trail, it is much easier and cheaper to use brochures for the trail interpretation. On the other hand, if 6,000 visitors a year walk the trail, the cost of printing brochures for each visitor could exceed the cost of having signs-in-place. In this case, having signs might be more cost effective. You can figure out the cost per visitor contact for each media (generally spread over five years), and quickly see which one is the most cost effective.

When

When do you think visitors will actually be walking this trail? For example, if its main use is only in the summer, there is no need to interpret wildflowers that bloom during other seasons. If the trail is going to be used year-round, then you may need "seasonal" interpretive media, such as distinct trail guides for spring/summer and fall/ winter. When planning for this concern look at your visitor use patterns, and at the resource itself. I have helped plan some trails in the East where, even though most visitors come to the park in summer, bugs keep most visitors away from the trails, using them mostly in spring or fall. I have worked on trails in the West and in the desert where it is too hot for visitors to walk trails in summer, except perhaps during early mornings or late evenings. Consider this kind of analysis for your trails.

Where

This planning consideration is designed to help you with your trail location. I emphasized earlier the importance of putting the trail where your visitors can have easy access to it. But there are other considerations for deciding where to locate the trail. You need to walk the site and analyze its physical location and any events that might affect the trail, such as:

- If it is near a river or stream, will the trail flood seasonally? If it does, will trail coverings such as wood chips have to be replaced yearly? Should you use gravel or "natural" trail surfacing? Will any trail furniture (benches, bridges, steps) be affected by high water?
- If the trail goes through a wetland and you have to use a boardwalk, will seasonal changes in water levels inundate the boardwalk or leave it high and dry?
- If the trail is too steep, will older visitors, children, and visitors with disabilities be able to use it?
- Is the trail easily accessible from campgrounds, parking areas, etc.?

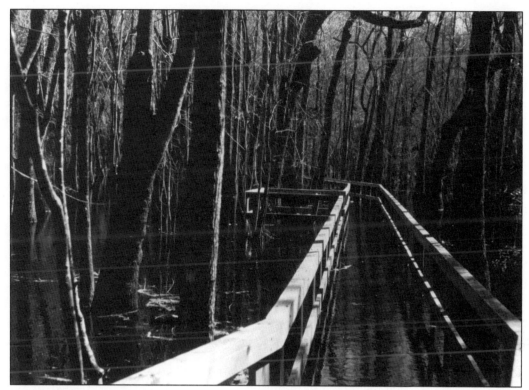

This boardwalk was planned in the fall when the water level was low. This photo was taken in spring.

Implementations and operations is the part of the trail plan where you have to figure out the costs for putting in the trail. This can include, but not be limited to:

- Staff time for trail layout and flagging.
- Staff time for cutting the trail.
- Costs for any trail drainage work (water bars).
- Costs for any steps, bridges, boardwalks.
- Costs for developing the trailhead area and related parking area.
- Costs for developing the trail media (signs, brochures, etc.)
- Cost for developing the trailhead sign.
- Need for trail maintenance (yearly, monthly?).
- Maintenance for trailhead area (parking lot), cost of litter pick up, etc.

Besides the costs, you have to figure out scheduling times (who can do what for you and when are they available to do it). I have found that the best way to handle I&O is to develop a check list of all the tasks to be done, with the cost for each.

So What

When all of the trail planning is over, what it all boils down to is this: "Are the objectives I set for the trail being accomplished?" In the evaluation section of this book I have provided a number of ways for you to do evaluations to see if the media and presentation are working as planned. If you take the time to pre-test your brochures, signs, or exhibits, you probably won't have too many problems with this. You knew they worked before you produced them in quantity.

As a general summary of the planning process, Figure 35 illustrates an Interpretive Planning Flow Chart for trails and self-guiding auto tours (and scenic byways).

Planning for Rehabilitation of Existing Self-guiding Trails

Quite often I take on projects where I am asked to "fix" an existing SGT, complete with its brochures or signs. The planning process I go through for this kind of project is exactly the same as for the new SGT, except the managerial realities are that a trail route exists. The basic planning process is the same as with new trails. Here are some main points to consider in rehab-trail planning:

- Do a new inventory of all interpretive resources along the existing trail, and map their locations on a trail map. This can include existing trail stops, as well as potential new ones.
- Do an analysis of the resources to determine the best theme for the trail. What story is the trail best able to illustrate?
- Map out your new trail stops along the existing trail. Remember, any existing trail stop markers or signs-in-place can be moved or removed as needed.
- Re-flag the trail to indicate the new trail stop locations.
- All other steps in the planning process remain the same.

Some General Rules For Planning SGTs

In planning SGTs, here are some general rules that I recommend:

- The best length for a SGT is between 1/2 and 3/4 miles long. General visitors can tire (and get bored) easily. If the trail is too long, visitors won't get past the halfway point before they notice how sore their feet are, all the bugs, and how hot it is. A short trail can give visitors a good trail experience without wearing them out in the process. This translates into a 45-minute to one-hour trail walk on basically level ground.
- A SGT should be on as level ground as possible to make the trail easily accessible to all visitors.
- A SGT should be easily accessible from campgrounds or other highly populated or well-used areas.

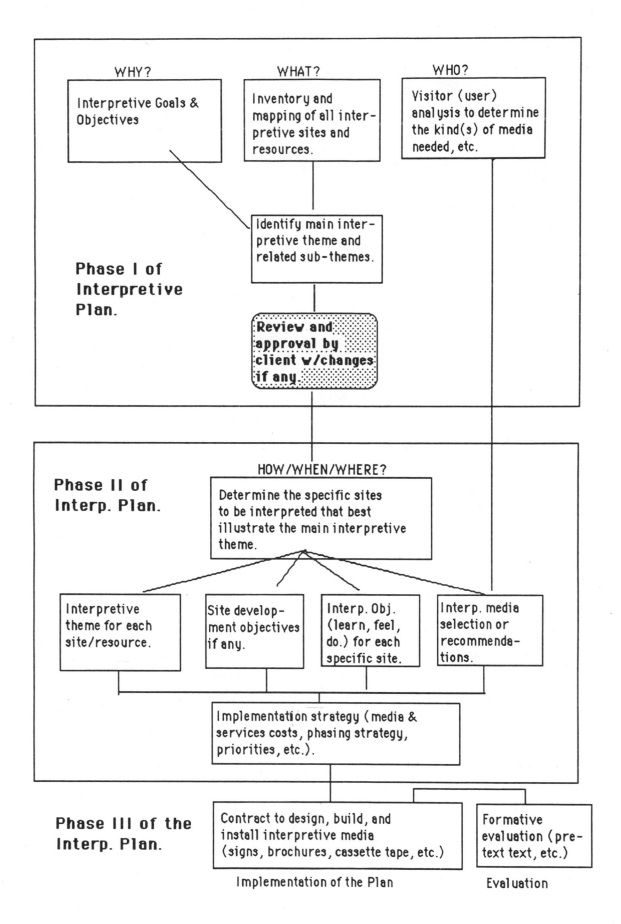

Figure 35.   **Interpretive Planning Flow Chart (Trails & Scenic Byways)**   JVA 1992

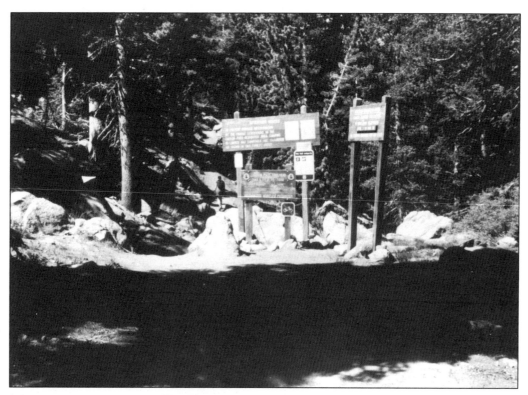

Care should be taken that trailhead areas are not over signed or cluttered looking.

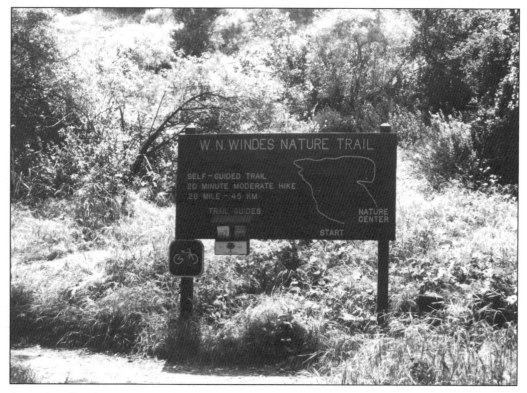

A good trailhead sign provides basic information about the trail route, walking time, safety, and visitor orientation.

- The best number of stops for an SGT is seven to ten. Too many stops wears people out. Remember, visitors are there for recreation and enjoyment, and to see the resource, not to read lots of interpretive text. Seven to ten stops on a 3/4-mile trail is plenty.
- An SGT should be a loop trail. Visitors like to know that they will end up close to where they started.
- Consider benches or other trail furniture along the trail as well. Where do you think people would like to sit and rest or simply enjoy the scenery?

The Trail Entrance Sign

All SGTs should have an easily recognizable trailhead area or starting point. In general here are a few things that all trailhead signs should have on them. Figure 36 is an example of a trailhead sign from the U.S. Army Corps of Engineers "Interpretive Graphics Standards."

- Give the name of the trail.
- Give a brief introduction to the trail and include an estimate of walking time. Most visitors have no idea how long a mile is, or how long it will take them to walk one mile on this particular trail.
- Include a map of the whole trail or trail system.
- Provide any safety information (watch for poison ivy, sturdy walking shoes are recommended, etc.).

Writing Interpretive Text for Signs or Brochures

After you have planned the trail and identified each of the seven to ten trail stops, the next thing you have to do is to "plan" each stop. By this I mean that you have to develop the specific objectives that you want each trail stop to accomplish. I usually write at least one learning, behavioral, and emotional objective for each trail stop. For example:

- The majority of visitors will be able to find fossils in the stream bed.
- The majority of visitors will learn how the fossils got in the stream bed.
- The majority of visitors will be amazed to learn that this area was once the bottom of an ancient sea bed.
- The majority of the visitors will learn not to pick up fossils.

The **objectives** will tell us what to research for the text and graphics for each stop. In this example, the graphics will need to show the visitor exactly what the "fossils" look like. The next may tell them exactly where to look along the stream bed to find the fossils. Research will be needed (with supporting graphics) to interpret how the fossils got here, and what this area may have looked like millions of years ago. Once you have your objectives, you don't have to guess what to write about.

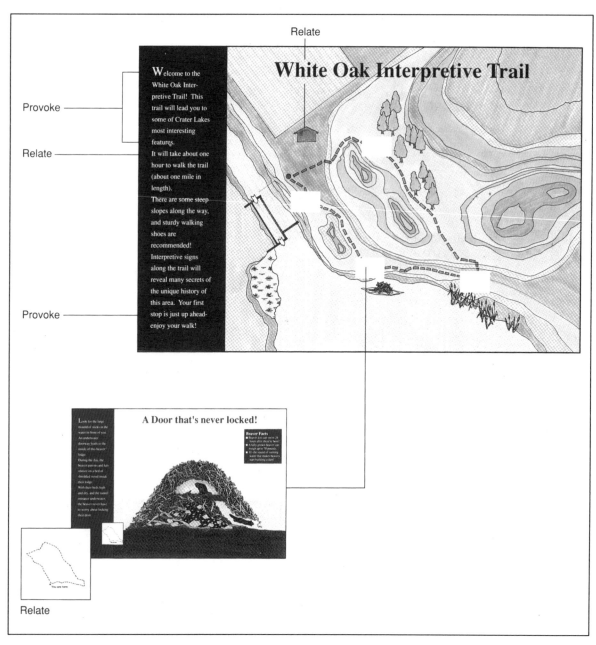

Figure 36. Trail head sign example from the U.S. Army Corps of Engineers "Interpretive Graphics Standards." Note how Tilden's principles are used in the panel.

Hints for Better Writing

- Keep the text short.

  We know from exhibit research that if the text is over fifty words long, it probably won't be read. For brochures, try not to have more than two short paragraphs of fifty words each. Ideally, I try to have one fifty-word paragraph and let the visuals do most of the work. Remember: visitors remember 30 percent of what they read and 50 percent of what they see.

- The text should be interpretive.

  That means the text should **provoke**, **relate**, and **reveal** the story being interpreted.

- Avoid using technical or professional jargon.

- Remember the behavioral objective.

  Have visitors "look for," "listen for," and "touch the..." in the text. Visitors will remember about 90 percent of what they do. Use the text to give them directions to DO something.

Here are some examples of texts from a self-guided trail brochure to illustrate these points.

Stop 1

Welcome to the Hidden Change Interpretive Trail!

This short 1/4-mile loop trail will only take about 35 minutes to walk. Look for the numbered stops along the way. They match the numbered stops in this trail guide. A constantly changing landscape now surrounds you, sculpted by the hands of fire and water. This process is called "succession," and the story begins just up ahead. Enjoy your walk.

Stop 2

How to Succeed Without Really Trying

The process of succession or change from one plant community to another is a never ending process. The community that is the last in the struggle for dominance is called the "climax" community. No other plants can out-compete this community for sunlight, food, or space. Look at the large pine and fir trees in front of you. They are a part of this forest's climax community.

A change on the way?

Will a climax community like this one remain unchanged forever? You'll find out the answer to this question just a little ways down the trail at Stop 3.

Stop 3

Scars of Change

Even a climax forest can change! When a forest fire burned through here years ago, many old, large trees were destroyed. Look around and imagine what it must have been like to see no trees or plants. The neighborhood changed, and the process of succession had to begin all over again. What do you think were the first plants to grow back after the fire? We'll show you at Stop 4.

What do you think the main interpretive theme and objectives were for this trail?

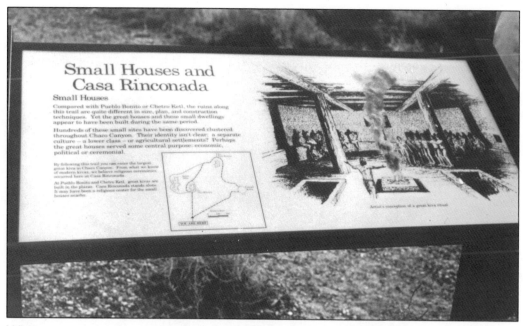

When you use a large typesize such as 36 point, 50 word paragraphs can take up a lot of room.

Planning for Signs-in-place for Self-guided Trails

The planning process for developing signs-in-place follows the same basic principles for interpretive planning. In general you should:

- Identify the objectives each sign-in-place has to accomplish. The learning objectives will tell you what to research or write about, and what kinds of illustrations you may need. The behavioral objectives will help you write copy so visitors will be asked to "look for..., listen for, find the..., touch the...," and so on. The emotional objectives will help you with the actual design of the sign—color selections, photograph choices, and graphic needs—to generate the emotions you have planned for.
- Identify the audience the signs will be designed for. Will you need large print for signs for older visitors? What vocabulary will you need to use? Remember the exercise from Chapter One on learning concepts and principles.
- Identify the kind of sign materials and mounting you want to use. What fabrication process will you use?
- Will you need any seasonally changing signs?
- What will different fabrication processes cost? How long will it take to have the signs made? Which materials are the most cost effective, the most vandal resistant? Who will write the copy, do the graphics, etc?

- Text length for trail signs-in-place should be about fifty words and not more than two fifty-word paragraphs. Use the largest text point size you can.

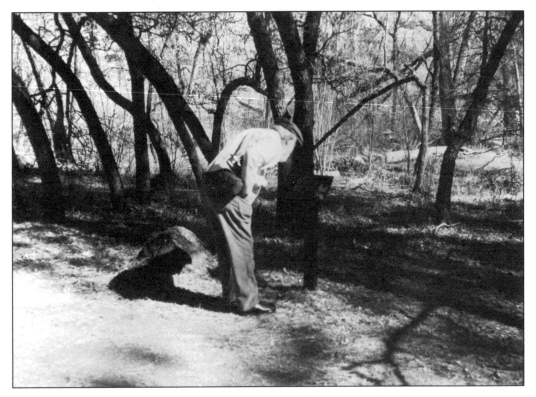

Visitors should never have to bend over or squint to read an interpretive sign.

- Monitor the vocabulary level you use. I usually write at a fifth-grade vocabulary level, but your word choice will depend on your audience. Remember interpretive pacing.
- Chose the photo or graphic that BEST illustrates the theme and accomplishes your emotional objectives. Don't waste money on "dumb graphics" that simply illustrate what the visitor can see in reality. For example, if the visitor is looking at oak trees, don't spend a lot of money having an artist do a graphic of an oak leaf. Illustrate concepts—not things.
- Try to design the sign to accomplish its objectives without using any text. Use text as the last resort. Why? Remember that visitors remember 30 percent of what they read, 50 percent of what they see, and 90 percent of what they do. If you have a lot of foreign visitors, graphics will be the most beneficial for them too.
- Use all of Tilden's Tips in the design and message presentation.

- **Pre-test the draft sign mock up to see if it works before you have the final sign fabricated.** Remember: it's the interpretive communication that's important, not what the message is printed on.
- Try to have some color if possible—it has "attraction power."
- The best size for most signs is 20 inches by 30 inches or larger.
- The trailhead sign needs to **provoke** (hook) the visitors into wanting to walk the trail.

Figure 37 gives some examples of interpretive trail signs from the U.S. Army Corps of Engineers "Interpretive Graphics Standards." I have noted along the margins of each sign how Tilden's Tips have been used.

Planning for Self-guiding Trail Brochures

The same process and points listed already for doing interpreting writing and for developing interpretive signs-in-place apply for developing the content for interpretive self-guiding brochures. The main difference is that instead of having seven to ten signs, you would have the same graphics or photo and the same text in one brochure. Here are some general points to remember:

- First impressions. The cover design is very important. It conveys to the visitor the essence of the story and provides provocation as well. It must have "attraction power."

You must also consider some design selections for the brochure:

- What color of paper should you use? What color relates best to your theme or message?.
- What paper weight should you use? Hint: heavier weight papers work best for brochures intended for outdoor use.
- What kind of paper texture should you use? Enamel paper that's shiny or non-glare paper? Which do you think is best for outdoors?
- What size of paper do you need for the brochure? How many folds will you need?
- What color(s) of ink should you use?
- What type face and size is best to use?
- How many photos or graphics do you need?
- Look back at the two examples and think about what's good or bad about each.
- How is the brochure designed to be marketed? Will it be given out at an information desk, or is it for a brochure rack? If it is for a brochure rack, perhaps at Highway Travel Information Stations, remember that usually only the top third of the brochure is visible in the rack.

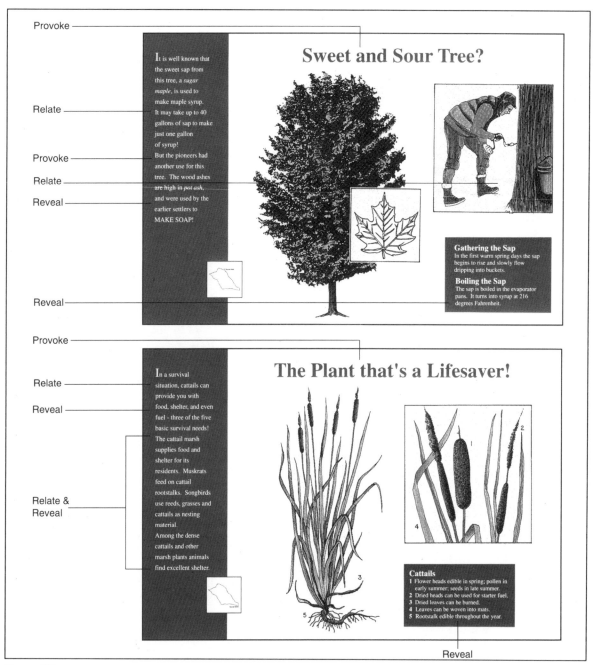

Provoke

Relate

Provoke

Relate

Reveal

Reveal

Sweet and Sour Tree?

It is well known that the sweet sap from this tree, a *sugar maple*, is used to make maple syrup. It may take up to 40 gallons of sap to make just one gallon of syrup! But the pioneers had another use for this tree. The wood ashes are high in *pot ash*, and were used by the earlier settlers to MAKE SOAP!

Gathering the Sap
In the first warm spring days the sap begins to rise and slowly flow dripping into buckets.

Boiling the Sap
The sap is boiled in the evaporator pans. It turns into syrup at 216 degrees Fahrenheit.

Provoke

Relate

Reveal

Relate & Reveal

The Plant that's a Lifesaver!

In a survival situation, cattails can provide you with food, shelter, and even fuel - three of the five basic survival needs! The cattail marsh supplies food and shelter for its residents. Muskrats feed on cattail rootstalks. Songbirds use reeds, grasses and cattails as nesting material. Among the dense cattails and other marsh plants animals find excellent shelter.

Cattails
1 Flower heads edible in spring; pollen in early summer; seeds in late summer.
2 Dried heads can be used for starter fuel.
3 Dried leaves can be burned.
4 Leaves can be woven into mats.
5 Rootstalk edible throughout the year.

Reveal

Figure 37.

Who Can Help You?

If you feel that you need some help, here are some places to check.

- Most quality print shops can help you with design and layout.
- Most federal agencies have public affairs specialists and design specialists who can help you.
- If you work in an agency, check to see which types of support services are available to you.

Planning for Self-guided Auto Tours

The planning process for SGATs is exactly the same as for planning interpretive trails with a few exceptions. Here are the main considerations I use for planning SGATs.

What

Auto tours generally will cover many miles and can take from one to several hours to complete. In doing an inventory to determine the best route for an auto tour, I generally consider:

- Where should the Auto Tour begin? Try to pick a location that can be easily found by visitors such as a concession area, campground, or visitor center. Then, on a topo map, do an inventory of all the main interpretive features that the visitor can see, just like with the SGT, but covering a greater area. Some of the things to look for include:

- Scenic vistas
- Demonstration areas
- Drive-by sites that don't require visitors to get out of their cars, such as interpreting the geology of a mountain range, or a particular land management program that may cover several miles of roadside viewing.
- Specific natural or cultural sites or features easily viewed from the road.

- Based on the resources, develop an interpretive theme for the SGAT.
- Then sketch out a route on a site map or topo map and drive the route to each of the intended interpretive sites. Note the mileage between each site on the map as you drive the route. Also note any road conditions, potential "confusion points" where visitors will need additional direction signs to keep on the right road, and potential safety hazards (like making a left turn across traffic, road pull-offs, etc.).
- Based on driving the route, make a final judgment as to the best (and safest) stops for the Auto Tour, which stops visitors can get out of their car and look around, which stops should be "drive-bys," and so on.
- Then drive the tour route again, noting the starting mileage and time, and note on the site route map the mileage between each stop. Write this down *now* because you will need it when you develop the text for the self-guiding brochure or tape for the Auto Tour.

Why

At the same time you do the field work on the tour, also work on developing the objectives that the client wants the tour to accomplish. Some examples might be:

- The majority of visitors will be able to see four different forest management techniques.
- The majority of visitors will have a greater appreciation of the management requirements of the special resources here.
- The majority of visitors will have a chance to learn about the cultural heritage of the valley by seeing historical ruins and historic sites first hand.
- All visitors will interact with the resources along the tour in a safe and responsible manner.
- The majority of visitors will have an increased appreciation for the complexities of managing such a large resource area.

Who

The WHO section of the SGAT plan tells you just what kind of tour you need. For example, you may have mostly single-day or weekend visitors using the tour. Or the SGAT may be just for visitors camping or visiting your area. One auto tour I designed for a national forest was targeted for tourists driving through the forest on a scenic byway. Depending on WHO the primary tour user will be, you will have to develop the route and text differently to meet the specific requirements of each different market group. The visitor analysis will give you ideas as to:

- How long to make the auto tour.
- What kinds of vehicles will probably be used (cars vs. campers vs. buses).
- Should the tour be a loop or a linear route?
- Should specific kinds of information be provided in the text based on any special interests of the visitors?

How

There are generally three media that are the most commonly used for self-guiding auto tours. These are self-guiding brochures, cassette tapes, and wayside exhibit panels. Many SGATs I have worked on have used two or more media, each with its own benefits. Let's take a closer at how to plan for each.

Self-guiding Auto Tour Brochures

Developing the brochure for an SGAT is the same as developing one for a trail. For each stop on the tour, write specific learning, behavioral, and emotional objectives that you want accomplished at each stop. Then develop the text, instructions, and graphic selections based on those objectives. The greatest difference between developing SGT brochures for trails and auto tours is that you have to provide more directions in the Auto Tour Brochure. Here are some things to consider for an SGAT brochure.

- Be sure that you have an accurate auto tour route map in the brochure.
- Give ample directions to the driver for how to find each stop and how to stay on the tour route. There is an international symbol for SGATs. Illustrate this in the brochure, and tell the driver to look for this tour route marking system along the roadway. Give mileage between stops so the driver will know when a designated stop is near. If the resource is a drive-by site, tell the driver that too.
- If possible, it is best to print the text for each tour stop and the directions for tour stops in different colors in the tour guide. This makes it easier for the visitors to use the tour guide.
- Make sure that you use Tilden's Tips (**provoke**, **relate**, and **reveal**) in developing the text for each stop.
- The seven-to-ten stop general rule doesn't apply to auto tours because you may be covering lots of territory. But make sure each stop illustrates your theme, just as with self-guiding trails.

Figures 38a and 38b are examples of the introduction and first stop from the SGAT I developed for Lassen National Forest. Note the use of the international SGAT logo, and the use of directions, which were printed in blue in the actual brochure.

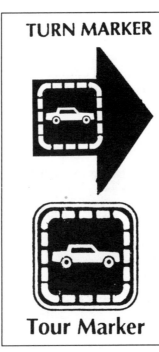

TURN MARKER

Tour Marker

Figure 38a.

Welcome! Do you know what a volcano, forest fire, and pronghorn antelope all have in common? They're some of many exciting things you'll see on your "Trip Through Time" self-guiding auto tour.

These symbols will be your guide for the tour route and will mark each stop. The tour route map will show you your location and the location of each stop as you travel. The tour is about 32 miles long, and will take about two to four hours to complete, depending on how long you want to spend at each stop. As there are no grocery stores along the route, you may want to take water and a snack with you.

To Begin: Start at the Christie Campground on Eagle Lake Road (Co. A1). Check your odometer; this booklet gives approximate distances to each stop. Enjoy your adventure!

Stop 1

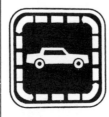

Gone in a Flash!

Look at the mountains on your left as you drive along. Can you see the fire scars on the mountain slope? Lightning struck here in 1955 causing a wildfire that burned an area bigger than downtown Los Angeles. The 19,000-acre fire was named the Merrill Burn. Growing new trees in the Merrill Burn area has been only partially successful due to competition from other plants for food and water. But in time, the mountain will be covered with trees again. How long do you think it will take?

Directions: Continue driving and watch for Tour Marker 2 on the right. This is a drive-by site, so you will not have to pull your car over or stop along the road.

Figure 38b.

Planning Wayside Exhibit Panels

One of the most common interpretive media for auto tours is using wayside exhibit panels. Planning for wayside exhibits is exactly the same as the outline presented for planning signs-in-place for self-guiding trails, with the exception that the panels are larger and can have a more random placement (Figure 39). In general you should:

- Determine the specific objectives that the panel has to accomplish.
- Determine the audience that will be viewing and interacting with the panel.
- Remember that the visuals are more important than the text. Remember to have some interaction built in (i.e. "look for..., listen for...," and so on).
- Usual size format is 2 feet by 3 feet.
- Keep the text to a minimum, not more than two fifty-word paragraphs.
- Best point size for the text copy is about 36 point. Remember, visitors should be able to easily read the text from several feet away. Veverka's Law Number 3: "Visitors should not have to bend over or strain their eyes to be able to read the exhibit copy."
- Remember to use all of Tilden's principles in the sign design and communication presentation.

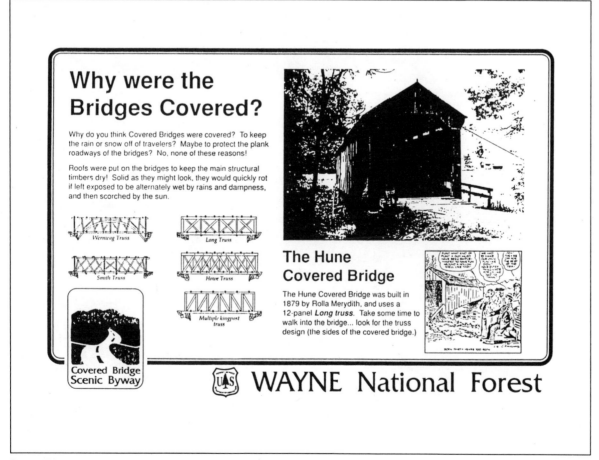

Figure 39.

Here are a few examples of wayside exhibit panels from the U.S. Army Corps of Engineers National Graphics Standards Manual (Figure 40).

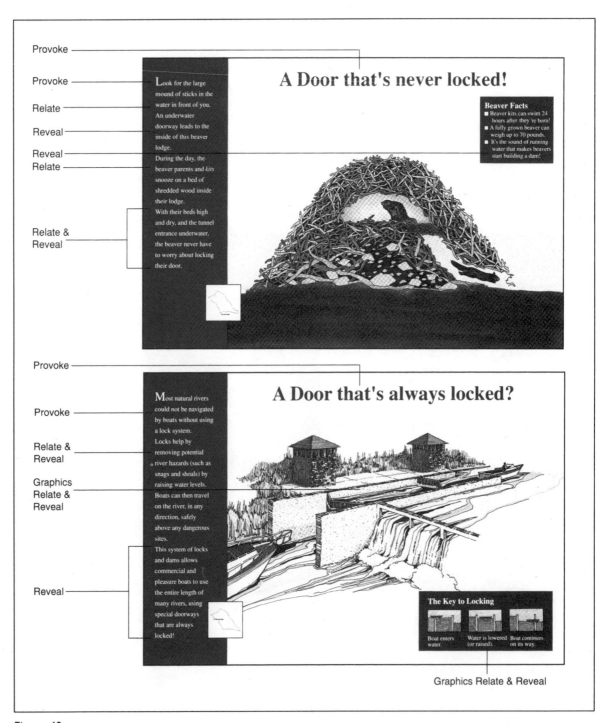

Figure 40.

Self-guiding Cassette Tapes

In developing a cassette tape for the auto tour, the first thing to remember is that the content will be the same as presented in written text for a brochure, and the objectives for each stop will be the same. Only the media has changed. Here are points to remember in developing an SGAT cassette tape.

- You will need a script for the narrator(s) to read. It should be written "the way people talk," using contractions (*you're* rather than you are) and plain language. Get a professional narrator to do the audio.
- You must plan in any need for sound effects and appropriate background music to support your message.
- You may want to consider using more than one voice. "Interview" other resource people or have them recite short segments on their areas of expertise. Having more than one voice on the tape makes it more interesting. But your main narrator should be a professional "voice."
- As with the tour brochures, you will need to give the driver directions to each stop. Try to avoid the BEEPS that are commonly used. There are other ways of making the transition. You can just have the narrator say "you can turn the tape off now and turn it on again when you see tour stop marker number 4."
- Remember the same rules apply about visitors remembering 50 percent of what they see and 90 percent of what they do. Have the narrator ask people to "look for..." and "try to find..." to have some active visitor involvement.
- Get the advice of professionals in developing the tape. You will need help with getting the professional voice, sound studio arrangements, sound effects mixing, background music selections mixing, etc.
- When you have a draft of the tape, drive the tour with it to see if it is accurate and whether the directions make sense.
- Remember, for it to be interpretive it must **provoke**, **relate**, and **reveal** the story to the visitor.
- Remember to provide directions to visitors on how to return the tape (if it was provided on loan).

Implementation & Operations

You will need to consider and plan for:

- How many copies of the tape will you want to have produced?
- How will you market the tape (have visitor learn about it)?
- Will it be for sale, or provided on loan? Where will the pick up and drop off points be?
- What will it cost to produce the tape, including a professional narrator, and all the required sound studio work?
- How long will the whole production take (from route planning to script development, to production of the final tape)? Hint: give yourself a year!

Evaluation

In the case of developing cassettes, due to the costs of making any corrections once the initial sound studio mixing has been done, I recommend doing formative evaluation. That is, pre-test the script, background music, etc. before you go into more elaborate studio production. You will be paying your professional voice $50-$100 an hour or more, so you don't want him or her to have to do lots of re-takes. Get the script to the point where the objectives for each stop are being met. Then have the professional narrator do the script on tape. Likewise, you can have other people evaluate the background music or sound effects to see if they accurately reflect the feelings or purposes for which the tape is intended. Once you have pre-tested these, and you know they will work well, then have them put in the tape so that all of the mixing is done at one time, combining the narration and the background effects.

Other techniques for evaluation are presented in Chapter Three.

References

Ham, S.H. 1992. *Environmental Interpretation: A Practical Guide for People with Big Ideas and Small Budgets.* Golden, CO: North American Press.

Gross, Michael, and R. Zimmerman. 1992. *Signs, Trails, and Wayside Exhibits: Connecting People and Places.* College of Natural Resources, University of Wisconsin-Stevens Point.

Parks Canada. 1978. *Trail Manual.* Engineering and Architecture Branch, Parks Canada, Ottawa.

Veverka, J.A. 1979. *Interpretive Trails and Related Facilities Manual.* Alberta Provincial Parks, Edmonton, Alberta, Canada.

Veverka, J.A. 1992. *U.S. Army Corps of Engineers Interpretive Graphics Standards Manual.*

Chapter Five

Planning for Interpretive Exhibits

abcdefghijklmnopqrstuvwxyz

In our interpretive centers we've got these arranged in ways that will make you cry, giggle, love, hate, wonder, and understand.

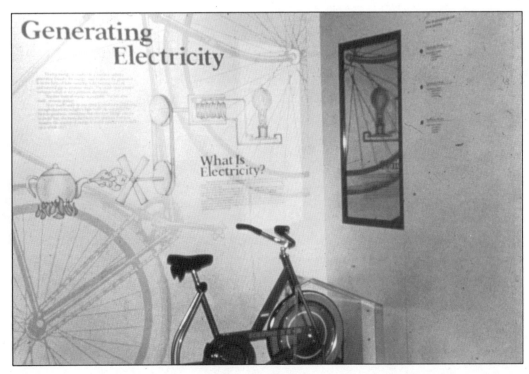

Take a closer look at your exhibits. Are they merely informational or are they truly interpretive?

Over the past few years most museums, nature centers, zoos, and other interpretive organizations have added the word *interpretive* to their exhibits. Many professional exhibit design and fabrication firms also note that they can develop interpretive exhibits. In the course of having been involved in formal planning, design, or evaluations or exhibits, I have noticed that many (most!) of the "interpretive" exhibits I have seen were not in the least sense interpretive. So what makes an exhibit interpretive, anyway? In this chapter, we will look at what's involved in the planning and design of exhibits, and ways to make sure your exhibits are indeed interpretive.

What is an Exhibit?

An exhibit is an array of cues purposely brought together within defined boundaries for a desired effect.

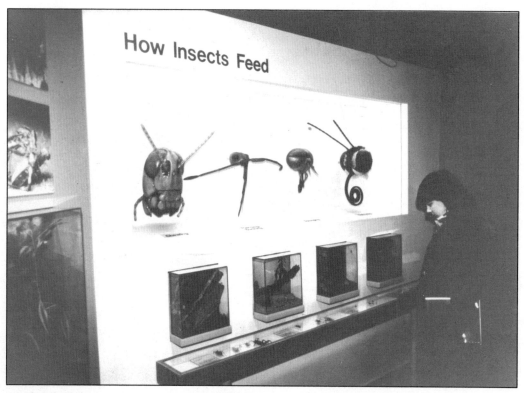

Exhibits can bring extremes into human scale.

Reasons for Exhibits

Sometimes planners forget that they might not need an exhibit to communicate a message to the visitor. Other forms of communication, such as self-guiding tours, publications, or guided programs, may be more effective. Here are some general reasons for having exhibits.

- To tell a story in an ordered sequence or fashion.
- To tell a story that cannot be told or illustrated on-site.
- To bring artifacts and stories to places where the people are.
- To incorporate and protect "real" artifacts.
- To bring extremes into human scale.
- To allow visitors freedom to pace themselves.
- To allow staff to do other things.
- To encourage visitors to see "the real thing" if and when possible.

What is an Interpretive Exhibit?

An exhibit is *interpretive* if it makes the topic come to life through active visitor involvement and extreme relevance to the everyday life of the viewer.

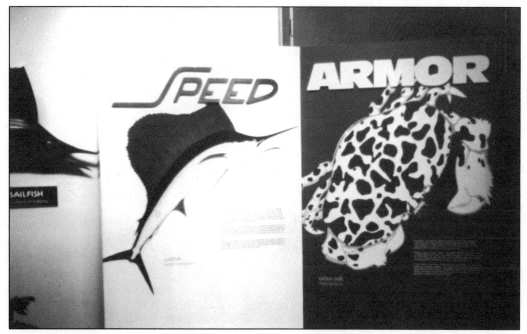

These two panels use good examples of "message unity." Does the graphic and header provoke your attention?

Characteristics of Interpretive Exhibits

So what makes an exhibit actually interpretive? If you remember back to Chapter Two's discussion of interpretive principles, nothing has changed. The same characteristics that make a self-guiding trail or a publication interpretive also apply to exhibits. Here is a summary of some of the main characteristics of interpretive exhibits.

They MUST employ interpretive techniques and principles.

- They must **provoke** interest or curiosity (otherwise no one will even stop to look at them).
- They must **relate** to the everyday life of the viewer.
- They should **reveal** the story through a unique ending or viewpoint.
- They should be part of a **theme** or story they are helping to illustrate, and fit into the big picture (remember the cow's head exercise at the beginning of the book?).

They must have a sense of context and relate to other exhibits within that context.

They should leave the visitor asking for more.

All of the learning principles and concepts presented in the first chapter also apply to exhibits. Here are a few you need to especially consider in planning interpretive exhibits:

- We all bring our pasts to the present.
- First impressions are especially important.
- My perception is not your perception.
- Simplicity and organization clarify messages.
- A picture can be worth a thousand words.
- People learn better when they're actively involved in the learning process.

Exhibit Classifications

Before we take a closer look at planning interpretive exhibits, it is important to have a good understanding of some basic exhibit planning and design principles. In general, there are four different kinds of exhibits, as illustrated in Figure 41.

Exhibit Classification Matrix

	Exhibit	
	motion	inert
active	1	2a
passive	2b	3

(Visitor mode)

Examples:
1— Seismograph, live animal, "hands-on device."
2a—Electronic exhibit where visitors push buttons.
2b—Viewing zoo animal, moving models.
3— Art, photographs, flat-work graphics

Figure 41.

In general, exhibits either have motion or they don't. And exhibits either actively involve the visitor or they allow the visitor to play a more passive role. Type 1 exhibits are those where the exhibit is active (has motion or can be manipulated in some way) and the visitor is active—the visitor can touch or manipulate the exhibit in some way. This is a typical interactive exhibit, or hands-on device. Examples include petting or holding a live animal, or pushing a button to turn on a video or to select an answer to a question.

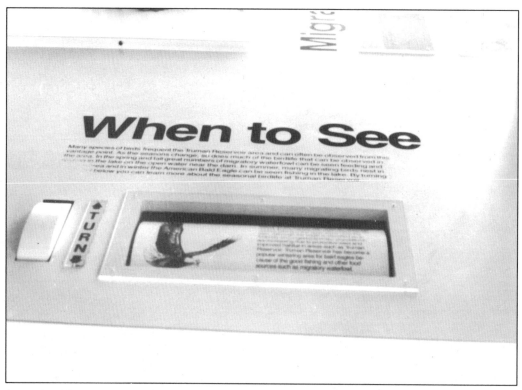

A type 1 exhibit. Note that the visitor must DO something and then the exhibit DOES something.

A type 2a exhibit is one where the visitor moves, but the exhibit is inert. This is any exhibit that has a hands-on activity, such as feeling an object or artifact on display.

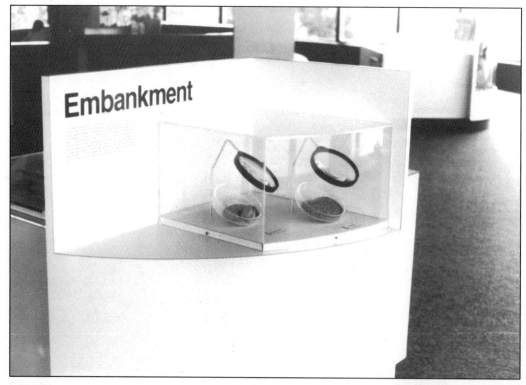

A type 2a exhibit. In this exhibit the visitor does all the moving to focus in on the soil samples.

Type 2b exhibits are ones where the visitor is passive, but the exhibit has motion, action, or animation of some sort. For example, watching fish in an aquarium is a type 2b exhibit.

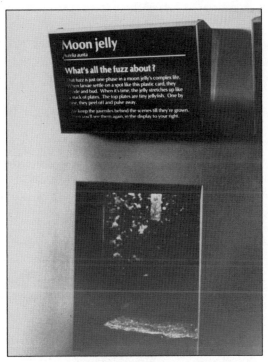

A type 2b exhibit. In this aquarium exhibit, the jellyfish larva do all the moving while the visitor stays still and watches.

With a type 3 exhibit visitor does nothing, and the exhibit does nothing back. This is typical of "flatwork" or collections. For example, most art museums present mostly type 3 exhibits.

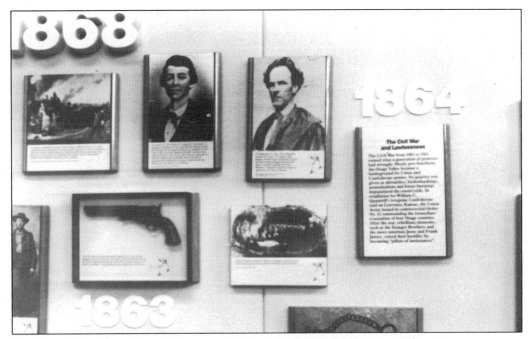

Type 3 exhibits. Flatworks exhibits generally have the least intrinsic interest for visitors.

The Concept of Exhibit Load

So what does this exhibit classification matrix, and the exhibit types (1, 2a, 2b, 3) have to do with anything? It forms the basis for understanding and using the concept of *exhibit load*. This is the term used to describe the amount of time and energy (either physical or emotional) that each exhibit requires from the visitor when interacting with it. Usually the highest load exhibits are the interactive ones (types 1, 2a, and 2b), and the low load exhibits are the most passive ones (usually type 3). The exhibit classification matrix gives one way to help determine the general load of an exhibit. I have given the type 2 exhibits an "a" and "b" notation, as in general I think that they have the same general load.

Another way to think of exhibit load is to imagine that a visitor enters an exhibit room with a gallon of enthusiasm or interest. Each exhibit encountered requires the visitor to use up some of that enthusiasm. Type 1 exhibits use the most emotional fuel, and type 3 exhibits use the least.

One of the things I try to do in planning interpretive exhibit galleries or rooms, is to build in "filling stations" within the exhibit area where visitors can get a second wind of enthusiasm and interest. Tilden's interpretive principles are very useful in doing this, as we shall see in the exhibit planning section of this chapter.

In addition, as the viewer goes from a type 1 to a type 3 exhibit there is a general decline in intrinsic interest for the less active exhibit. In addition, research has shown that people are more interested in dynamic, animated, changing stimuli than in inert flatwork. We also know that visitors have more intrinsic interest in real objects than in other forms of artifacts, such as replicas, as is shown in Figure 42.

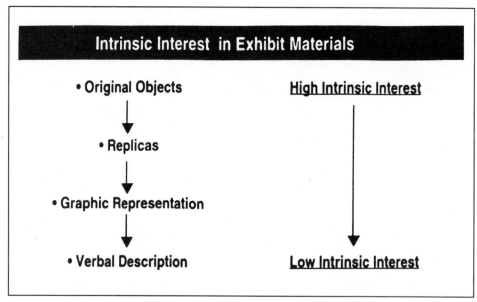

Figure 42.

As an example of this concept consider an exhibit on Davy Crockett's rifle.

Real Object. A display case with Davy Crockett's rifle in it. The visitor can imagine all of the places that this artifact has been, and the people and events associated with it. It a piece of real history, and a real story.

Replica. A display case with a replica of Davy Crockett's rifle. Looks like the real one, but has no story with it. It hasn't been anywhere, or done anything.

Graphic Representation. A display case or exhibit with a photograph of Davy Crockett's rifle. (Who cares?).

Verbal Description. Four hundred words of text describing Davy Crockett's rifle. Will anyone read it?

Mix and Match

The best plan of action, I have found, is to have a diversity of exhibit load types presented in a purposeful pattern. For example, an exhibit gallery might start with a type 2 exhibit slowly building the story up to a type 1 exhibit. The graph shown in Figure 43 illustrates a good pattern for your exhibit load.

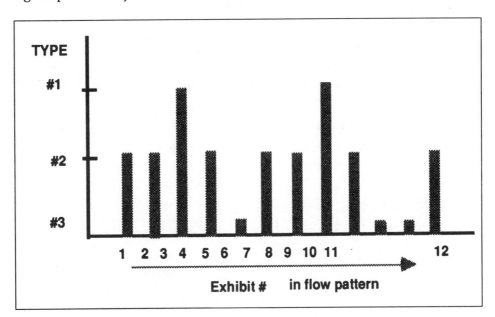

Figure 43.

Mapping Your Exhibit Load

This technique is very useful for predicting potential trouble areas in your exhibit room. If you have existing exhibits in the room, or have an exhibit plan that notes where each exhibit will be located in the room, you can map your exhibit load on the floor plan as shown in the example (Figure 44) on the next page.

In this floor plan we can see several things happening and perhaps make some design

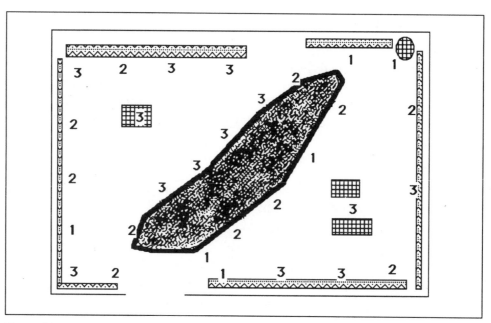

Figure 44.

changes. Note the type 1 exhibit at the entrance. It's best not to have interactive exhibits at the entrance to a gallery, or in areas where visitor flow through the room is tight. Why? Type 1 exhibits generally have more holding power, and the potential for a log jam in your visitor flow is greatest at these areas. Note the wall of type 3 exhibits. We call these "exhibit runways" because that's about how fast visitors will move down them and past the exhibits. Also note the type 1 exhibits across from the type 3 exhibits.

Where do you think the visitors will be drawn to and spend the most time? Figure 45 illustrates how you can predict potential visitor flow based on exhibit load. Note how the high load exhibits pull visitors away from the low load exhibits. You can use this technique as one of many tools to help you plan what will happen, physically, in your exhibit room.

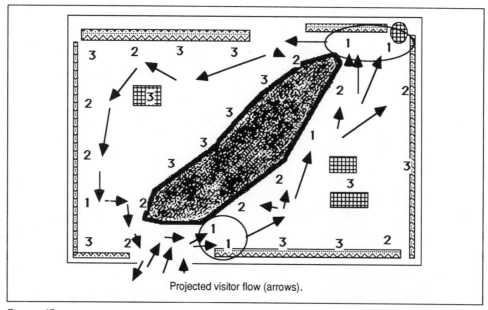

Projected visitor flow (arrows).

Figure 45.

Chapter Five Planning for Interpretive Exhibits

Planning
Interpretive Exhibits

With this general background on exhibits and exhibit types, let's look now at how to plan interpretive exhibits for a visitor center, interpretive center, or museum.

Remember the Visitor?

There is one thing that many (most) of the exhibits that I have seen in museums or interpretive centers have in common—the visitor was not taken into account at all in the planning of the exhibition or individual exhibit. The exhibits were designed for the curator, biologist, forester, or other resource expert with little regard for how the visitor learns or remembers information, or whether the visitor would even be interested in the subject matter being presented. In planning exhibits, the two main questions we usually ask in interpretive planning are quite important here, and must be asked and answered if the exhibit planner actually wants the visitor to learn or remember anything from the exhibit. Those two questions are:

1. Why would a visitor want to know this?
2. How do I want the visitor to USE the information being shared or interpreted to them?

Things to Remember About Visitors and Exhibits

From my experience in planning exhibits and doing evaluations of existing exhibits, there are several concepts that I have learned and observed in action in museums and interpretive centers. Here are a few of them:

- If an exhibit label is more than fifty words long, it probably will not be read by the visitors. Visitors generally are not interested in reading— they'd rather look at the artifacts or push some buttons. Exhibit labels are one of the few things that you can ask visitors to read standing up. And the smaller the text the more uninteresting the label becomes.

- If you can't communicate the main concept of the exhibit to the visitor in about fifteen seconds, you're probably not going to. Visitors generally do not spend much time at any one exhibit. If you want to find this out for yourself, see the evaluation section of this chapter.

- Provocative headlines and graphics will draw attention. Remember Tilden's Tips? Visitors will be drawn to exhibits that have information or artifacts of intrinsic interest to them (**relate**).

- The average viewing time for a video or slide program that is part of an exhibit is about three minutes. If you have a program longer than that, the visitors will probably not stand through the whole thing.

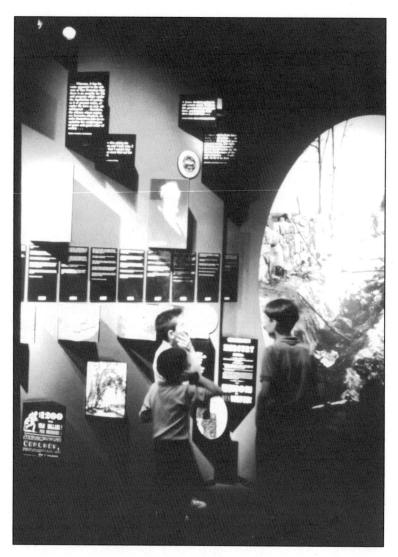

This is a classic example of exhibit sensory overload. Notice where the labels are located. Can you figure out the main point here?

- The average maximum time that visitors are willing to sit through a theater program in a visitor center or museum is about seven minutes. After that, attention and interest drop dramatically.

- Beware high-tech exhibits that can't be fixed by staff or that require odd parts unavailable at your local hardware store. Such exhibits tend to require frequent and costly maintenance.

- Evaluate the exhibits while in the design phase to judge whether their objectives are being met before you spend the money to build the actual exhibit.

- I usually write my labels at a fifth-grade vocabulary level. I have found that this is the vocabulary that best reaches ALL visitors. This is NOT talking down to visitors. Too often the text is full of specialized resource or professional jargon. Write the text so everyone can understand it (and so it **relates** to the everyday life of the visitor).

A 1989 publication by Region 8 of the USDA Forest Service entitled "Being Up Front and Out Front... Communicating through Interpretation" contains some "exhibit survey results" from the fall of 1987. The statistics were from two years of studies done by the USDA Design Division at nine different locations including the Adirondack New York Museum; the Smithsonian Air and Space Museums, the Begich-Boggs Visitor Center in Alaska; the Keowee-Toxaway Energy Complex Visitor Center in South Carolina; and the Williamsburg Visitor Center in Virginia. Here are some of the more interesting results from this two-year study.

1. Less than 1 percent of the people read the entire exhibit copy. Of this 1 percent, approximately 90 percent were either experts or researchers that already had a thorough knowledge of the subject matter.

2. The longer and more complex the written or recorded message, the shorter the viewing and listening time.

3. The average visitor spent only about 30 percent of the time actually needed to thoroughly view an exhibit and read the message.

4. Sixty-five percent of the visitors interacted with audience-participation devices. If the exhibit game was difficult or made an obvious point of a viewer mistake, they quickly moved away.

5. Thirty-five percent of the visitors viewed a three-dimensional topo map of the area. The retention of information or features was almost nothing.

6. Twenty-five percent viewed flat or graphic maps. Retention of roads and features was about double that for a topo map.

7. Thirty-seven percent listened to tape messages. Length of time was approximately four minutes. Messages nearly ten minutes long were listened to by only 5 percent of the visitors. Almost 95 percent of the listeners waited for the entire message if it was less than three minutes long.

8. Slide shows, videos, or movies were viewed by 55 percent of the visitors. Length again was a factor for viewing, as only 8 percent watched programs over six minutes long.

9. Taxidermy mounted animals that could be touched were handled by 94 percent of the visitors. Any touchable item increased participation over 90 percent.

10. Computer usage for games and information is on the up-swing. But program costs, maintenance, and lengthy delays for repairs are problems. The Keowee-Toxaway Center uses large numbers of computer games but had more than half of them inoperable. Keowee-Toxaway personnel wish they had never installed their eleven games because the first day was the only time they were all operable.

11. In over 90 percent of the sites and people surveyed the most important element of visitor contact was a competent and highly trained visitor staff. Everyone stressed the need for and difficulty of having and maintaining a professional visitor staff.

The main point here is that there is more to having a successful exhibit than putting "stuff on a wall" or "stuff in a box" and expecting visitors to be excited about it. All interpretive planners and exhibit planners need to be aware of the information that is available about visitors and their needs, interests, and how they learn and remember information in a "recreational learning environment."

How I Plan Interpretive Exhibits

My main planning approach for interpretive exhibits is the same planning strategy I use for planning all interpretive media. Remember in your planning that an exhibit must:

1. Be able to attract the visitor to it.
2. Be able to hold the visitor's attention after the initial attraction to it.
3. Be able to engage the visitor (get them to want to look at the visual cues and read the copy).
4. Effectively communicate with the visitor (the objectives of the exhibit—learn, feel, do—must be accomplished for genuine communication to occur).

With this in mind, let's do a walk through of a typical interpretive exhibit planning project for an interpretive center exhibit room.

What

Start the project by conducting what I call a "focus" workshop. The purpose of the workshop is to make sure that all planning team participants agree on what the main subject areas of the exhibition should be. What are the main interpretive theme and sub-themes? Ask the key question of each workshop participant: "If a visitor came into the center, looked at all of the exhibits, and then left...if the visitor remembers only one concept from the exhibit room, what do you want that one thing to be?"

As each person in the group contributes his or her "one main concept," write it on a large flip-chart pad. After about the fifth idea you will start to get repeats ("mine is like number three"). Once all of the main ideas are in, do a bubble diagram to visually look for the relationships of the ideas contributed. A typical bubble diagram is shown in Figure 46.

From the bubble diagram it is often easy to see the main theme and supporting sub-themes. Note the main interpretive theme for this exhibition. All other exhibits must, in some way, illustrate or support this theme.

The relationships between topics from the bubble diagram reveal what the main exhibit areas should be, and what should be the subject matter of each. For example, one sub-theme may take up one wall in the exhibit room.

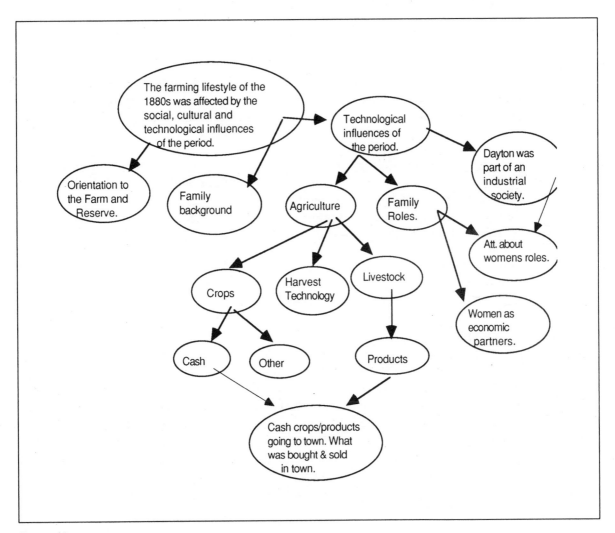

Figure 46.

Why

The goals and objectives for interpretation of the visitor center exhibit area should be reviewed prior to the focus workshop, and then modified or added to after the focus workshop. Here are some examples of interpretive objectives for the entire exhibition.

- All visitors will be encouraged to visit the actual working farm site after leaving the interpretive center.
- All visitors will be made aware of current or future programs or special events at the farm, and invited to attend them.
- All children will have the opportunity to take part in activities that were common to the 1880s farm life.
- The majority of visitors will understand the main interpretive theme for the farm and interpretive center exhibits.
- The majority of visitors will want to learn more about farm lifestyles of the 1880s.

Who

Always spend as much time as possible to identify the main target groups who will be using the center and interacting with the exhibits. This kind of data helps in planning the content presentation of the exhibits (so you can better **relate** to the visitors). You can determine if you need exhibits at different presentation levels (for adults and children, or text in other languages, etc.).

The audience analysis also reveals visitor use patterns. Will the visitors be seasonal visitors, on vacation, or will there be frequent use by local residents? If the exhibits will be used mainly by local or regional visitors (high numbers of repeat visitors), that means you should plan for more changing exhibits (for seasonal changes, as well as topic changes).

As with the other planning strategies, we do the WHAT, WHY, and WHO sections of the plan concurrently.

Story Line Development

After the goals and objectives of the exhibition have been determined, and the focus workshop reveals what the main theme and sub-themes for the exhibits will be, the next step is to write a story line walk through. This is like an expanded content outline of all of the exhibit areas, from the first "welcome" exhibit, to the final "summary" exhibit. It gives the exhibit planning team a chance to see if any topics have been left out, or if any topics suggested need not be part of the exhibit (given limited space for each exhibit). An example of one page from a story line walk through from the Carriage Hill Farm Visitor Center Interpretive Exhibit Plan is presented in Figure 47.

After the story line walk through has been approved, the next step is to develop the proposed content of each exhibit. Using standardized exhibit planning forms, draft the specific concept each exhibit should address and list the learning, behavioral, and emotional objectives of each exhibit. Sketch out some suggestions for exhibit presentations. An example of my exhibit planning work sheets from the Carriage Hill Farm Visitor Center is shown in Figures 48a and 48b.

When the planning forms have been completed and approved by the team, the interpretive exhibit plan is completed. The main theme, sub-themes, and the objectives for each and every exhibit are defined. When the exhibits are finally designed and built, no exhibit need be left out because of budget (no part of the story is left out). The plan is the story the exhibits are to illustrate. They can be illustrated in both expensive (type 1) exhibits, or less expensive exhibits (type 3), as budget and space allow for.

The beauty of the interpretive exhibit planning process is that you don't have to guess what the exhibits should be about. And when you receive draft designs of the exhibits, you have something by which to evaluate each draft design—the objectives for the exhibit.

The plan also helps the designer of the exhibit project. He or she doesn't have to guess what text is needed, what graphics or artifacts are needed to illustrate the story, or guess what feelings each exhibit should bring out in the visitor. This helps reduce the design time greatly.

Remember, the planning forms are tools for the planner, a convenient place to record data. Feel free to add to or change the format or content of these forms if you wish to use them for your next exhibit project.

The Exhibit Planning and Design Team

The most successful projects have the best teams. If you are going to be working on an exhibit project for a new or existing facility, I recommend that the planning team be formed and stay together throughout the project, even if some of the team members work or input is needed in only part of the planning and design process. The team members should include:

Interpretive Planner
Interpretive Exhibit Designer (if going on to design and build the exhibits right away)
Resource Specialists (historians, biologists, wildlife specialists, geologists, etc.)
Agency planner/project manager
Building architect (for new facility)

Story Line Walk Through

Project: Carriage Hill Farm

Exhibit	Theme	Details
	1. Discover CH Reserve & Farm	Map of the Reserve Signage to guide visitors Receptionist P.D. Identification P.D. and CH brochures Current programs Volunteer promotion AV Show
	2. Real People in Real Time at a Real Place.	
	a. Generations on the land.	Genealogy Brochure about family.
	b. Property Time Line	Who & When owned CH 1880s identified
	c. Empty Cradle	Death as 19th Cent. Reality.
	d. Impact of Religion	Church influenced choices in archetecture, clothing, furnishings, decoration and social life.
	e. We are as one Family	The extended family
	3. Technology	
	a. Changes through time.	Follow evolution of grain harvesting for example. Mixture of old & new tech. at any one time.
	b. 1880s Age of Technological Innovation.	Examples from the period of farm and household objects.

Figure 47.

EXHIBIT PLANNING WORKSHEET

PROJECT# CHF-92-3

Client: Dayton Montgomery Parks
Project: Carriage Hill Farm Visitor Center

Exhibit #: 2
Theme: The Arnolds' were not a typical Victorian farm family.
Exhibit Title:
The beginning Carriage Hill Farm.

Main Concept to be Interpreted:

The main concept for this exhibit group would be to introduce visitors to the Arnold family, and give them a general background at to who the family was, where they came from, etc., and to make visitors that they (and this farm) were not typical of Victorian farm families of the 1800s Dayton.

Exhibit Objectives

Learning Objectives:

The majority of visitors will gain a general introduction to, and overview of the Arnold family history.

The majority of the visitors will learn that when the Arnolds arrived, there were already two buildings here.

The majority of the visitors will learn the more recent history of the farm, with the Park buying the property, reconstruction, and restoration.

The majority of the visitors will learn the main philosophy and reasons as to why the park system is developing this farm.

Behavioral Objectives:

The majority of the visitors will want to go to the farm and see the buildings, and learn more about the farm.

The majority of the visitors will want to take part in farm activities (as available).

Emotional Objectives:

All visitors will feel that visiting the farm will be exciting and fun.

Figure 48a.

Exhibit Planning Worksheet

Exhibit #: 2

Audience:

All Carriage Hill visitors.

Materials to be used for/in the exhibit:

Historic pictures of the Arnold family.
Excerpts from Diaries.
Select family artifacts.
Map showing where the Arnold family came from.
Time line of property ownership.

Exhibit Presentation Ideas:

This exhibit group could use a variety of graphics and super graphics to illustrate the Arnold Family, and how they were not a typical Victorian farm family. An audio (digital sound) recording of someone reading from the family diary, or providing an audio overview of the family's history, with appropriate background music would be desired.

Could make elements of the exhibit interactive with questions "Why do you think the Arnolds were not a typical farm family?" with lift up flaps with answers under them.

Probably only a small amount of space would be needed for this exhibit section, as the family will be interpreted in more detail "on site".

Figure 48b.

What Will it Cost, How Long Will it Take?

One of the first mistakes most agencies make when planning exhibits for a new or existing facility is under-estimating what the project will cost and how long it will take. After having worked with a number of exhibit design firms for the past ten years, here are my general ideas about how to estimate costs for a typical interpretive center exhibit project.

The cost estimates begin with the square footage of the exhibit area(s). This is the floor space, not wall space. As of this writing most exhibit design firms use a general rule of thumb for estimating exhibit costs. That is an average cost of $200 per square foot for the complete planning, design, and fabrication of exhibits for a given area. So if you have 1,000 square feet of exhibit space, don't be surprised if your exhibit cost estimates runs about $200,000. This includes a mix of type 1 and type 3 exhibits. The less money you have to spend, the less type 1 exhibits you will have (they are the most expensive).

Here is how your exhibit budget generally breaks down. Approximately 20 to 25 percent of the total amount is for the planning and design of the exhibits. Another 10 to 15 percent is for delivery and installation of the exhibits in the center or facility. That leaves about 65 percent of your total budget for actual exhibits.

This is for a design and build budget, where one firm does the design and constructs the exhibits. If you break the contract into two separate contracts, one for design and one for construction, you must ask the designer to develop "bid documents" with very detailed design plans so a fabrication company can accurately estimate the costs for construction. This option, while a valid one, has some drawbacks. Here are a few of them.

- If something in the exhibit (like a high-tech, interactive exhibit) breaks or works poorly, who do you ask to fix it or replace it? I know of several examples where the client had a lot of exhibits that didn't work well at all. The designer said that the builder didn't follow the design drawing correctly. The builder said that they followed the design drawings exactly...they were just bad designs. The client can be stuck in the middle.
- It will add as much as 10 to 15 percent extra to the design costs for a designer to have to do a design "bid package."
- You will lose time and have a lot of extra money tied up in overhead in developing "Request for Proposals or Quotations," interviewing prospective contractors, and developing new contracts for the fabrication. This may add three or four months to the total project time line, not to mention the in-house overhead costs.
- It will add to your agency's contract cost—in preparation, bidding processes, and inspection.

The Overall Exhibit Plan, Design, and Build Process

If you will be doing your exhibit project from plan to installation, here is a general list of tasks that need to be done during or after the interpretive exhibit planning process (from Deaton Museum Services, Minneapolis, MN).

1. Establish the main theme (from the interpretive plan).
2. Establish the budget.
3. Prioritize topics within the exhibit (how much space and money will be spent on each exhibit topic or sub-theme?).
4. Conduct research based on stated themes and topics.
5. Review artifact collection, graphic materials, and other potential exhibit elements.
6. Write the exhibit outline (story line walk through).
7. Create a schematic plan.
8. Write a story line (done in exhibit interpretive plan).
9. Develop exhibit concept designs (based on objectives).
10. Continue research based on the story and exhibit concept (from objectives stated on interpretive exhibit planning forms).
11. Locate all artifacts and graphic originals and create a data sheet file.
12. Write the final exhibit label copy (use Tilden's principles).
13. Complete exhibit detail and graphic design.
14. Obtain graphic originals and artifacts and collect specimens for each exhibit.
15. Produce engineering and construction drawings.
16. Fabricate exhibit: casework, models, audio-visual programs, and graphic material.
17. Install the exhibit.
18. Mount artifacts.
19. Open to the public.
20. Evaluate. (Are general objectives being met? Are there flow problems, design problems, etc.?)
21. Make necessary modifications and revisions.

Contracting for Interpretive Exhibits

In general, most agencies will contract out with an exhibit firm to help them with their exhibit projects, sometimes just for the interpretive plan, the design, or the fabrication, or any combination of these steps. If you're not sure how to find the "best" interpretive exhibit design firm for your needs, here are some suggestions for when you write your "request for proposals" or for your project.

- At least one member of the firm should have at least a B.S. or M.S. degree in interpretation, or five years of experience in the interpretive field. This holds true particularly for the person who will be doing the interpretive plan, helping develop objectives, and writing any label copy. They should be totally fluent in interpretive principles and techniques. Ask for evidence of this. There is a big difference between "interpretive" exhibits and "trade show" exhibits.
- Ask them to send you some photographs or slides of the "best" interpretive exhibit that they designed (along with the objectives for that exhibit). Ask for a written narrative on "why the exhibit is interpretive."
- Talk to other agencies who have had recent interpretive exhibit projects done for them. Get a copy of their RFP's and a list of the firms they sent them to. How did they make their final selections?
- Check with the National Association for Interpretation. Most of the best "interpretive" exhibit firms are members of NAI, and you can get a list of these firms to contact for proposals.

There are lots of excellent interpretive exhibit planning and design firms out there. These ideas can help you find the best one for your project.

References

Ham, Sam H. 1992. *Environmental Interpretation: A Practical Guide for People with Big Ideas and Small Budgets*. Golden, CO: North American Press.

Veverka, J.A. 1990. *U.S. Army Corps of Engineers Interpretive Services Manual*.

Veverka, J.A. 1992. "Where is the Interpretation in Interpretive Exhibits." Occasional Paper, JVA Training Division.

Chapter Six

Planning Conducted Interpretive Programs

Play is what I do for a living; the work comes in
evaluating the results of the play.
- Mac MacDougall, Computer Architect

Some people have ideas. A few carry them into the world of action
and make them happen. These are the innovators.
- Andrew Mercer, Innovator

Clearly, the area of conducted activities (or personal services) represents the very essence of what interpretation is all about. The best developed conducted activity brings into play all five of the visitor's senses, permitting the visitor to be actively involved with the subject of the interpretive program. Undoubtedly, conducted activities are the most popular and effective interpretive media we can offer to the public.

Before we explore the basics of planning and delivering conducted programs or activities, let's first turn our attention to why people participate in such programs (from Lewis, 1988).

- To learn something they otherwise wouldn't.
- To make the unfamiliar familiar.
- To satisfy curiosity.
- To meet other visitors in a relatively intimate setting.
- To have an aesthetically pleasing experience.
- To be moved, touched, or inspired by the program or message.

Remember what we discovered in Chapter One about how people learn? Here is a short summary.

- People learn better when they're actively involved in the learning process.
- People learn better when they're using as many senses as appropriate.
- Each person has unique and valid ways of processing information and experiences.
- New learning is built on a foundation of previous knowledge.
- People prefer to learn that which is of most value to them at the present time.
- People learn best from first-hand experiences.
- Using a variety of approaches enhances learning.

Planning Your Program or Activity

By this time you should be anticipating the planning process. It will follow the same steps we used for all of the other media planning.

What

What is the main theme (or sub-theme) for your site or agency that your program has to help illustrate? How will your program help illustrate this main theme or story? What is your theme for this specific program? Remember that a theme is a simple complete sentence. Here are a few examples of program themes:

- All life is dependent on the sun.
- Mosquitoes are fascinating insects.
- Preserving habitats benefits animals, plants, and all of us.
- Snakes are important creatures.
- The early settlers had remarkable ways to use the natural resources they found around them.
- Ancient pottery is a window into the past.

Remember that you should not be able to ask the question "what about it?" after a theme statement. For example: "Birds of the Park." What about the birds of the park? This is a topic, not a theme.

Once you have your theme the rest of the program will fall quickly into place. Why? Because the program plan is based on how you will illustrate your theme; what kind of slides, artifacts, tour stops, etc. you will need to use.

Why

Develop the specific learning, behavioral, and emotional objectives that you want your program to accomplish. You don't have to write lots of objectives. Keep it simple. Answer yourself this—"If after my program the visitors only remember three things, those three things better be....." Fill in the blank and you've found some of your objectives.

Examples of objectives:

> **Learning objective:** The majority of the visitors will be able to tell me three ways they can improve habitats for wildlife at their own home.
> **Emotional objective:** The majority of the visitors will feel excited about improving habitats for wildlife at their home, and will want to try it when they get home.
> **Behavioral objective:** The majority of visitors will do some positive wildlife habitat improvement at their home within the next year, such as put up a bird feeder.

VERY IMPORTANT—as you think about the theme for your program, and the specific objectives that you want the program to accomplish, ask yourself these two questions:

1. Why would a visitor want to know that (or care)?
2. How do I want them to use the information I am giving them?

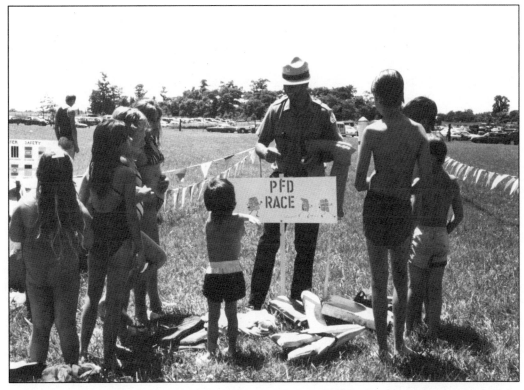

Interpreting water safety at a corps of engineers project site. What do you think the program objectives are?

Try not to have a program that gives lots of answers to questions that nobody is asking. The answer to the first question will give you ideas for marketing and advertising your program—telling potential program attendees why they should come to the program (the value of attending the program). What's in it for them!

The answer to the second question is your behavioral objective for your program, and in my mind, the most important objective to have accomplished.

Who

Who are the visitors (the target audience) for which you will be preparing and presenting the program? What special ways will you need to **relate** to them? How many visitors will be attending your program? Some things to consider:

- Space requirements for visitors (how many can you accommodate?).
- Ages of visitors.
- Interests of visitors.
- How much time do the visitors have for the program (how long will they want to stay)?
- How will you advertise the program—to which market groups?
- Will the program be too difficult (physically) for some visitors, such as a hike on a long and rugged trail?
- Can visitors easily find the program site?
- If it is a special group, do they have their own program objectives?
- Will they be interested in your program topic (why would they want to know...)?

How/When/Where

This part of the program plan is basically the logistics for the program.

How will the program be presented?

- By the interpretor
- By a guest speaker
- On a guided or led tour
- In a live demonstration
- Using slides or other media
- Through living history
- Other means

When will the program or activity be presented?

- One time only
- Once a week
- By request for groups only
- Offered several times a week
- Program starting and ending times

Where will the program or activity be presented?

- Indoors
- Outdoors
- At an interpretive facility
- In the wilds
- Where should visitors meet?

Implementation and Operations

This is the part of the program plan where you can make a list of all the things you will need to do or have to present the program. One of the best ways is to make a check list. Here is a partial check list for a slide program presentation:

Preparation

_____ Have you clearly written the objectives of your presentation?

_____ Have you analyzed your audience?

_____ Have you prepared an outline, organizing your talk around a theme and representing ideas in a smooth sequence?

_____ Have you researched your supporting information for accuracy and anticipated questions?

_____ Have you carefully selected slides that are relevant and of good composition and quality?

_____ Have you practiced your presentation and checked for slide sequence and timing as well as for smooth delivery?

_____ Did you give the program an interesting but understandable title?

_____ Does your program need additional materials to be shown or handed out?

_____ Have you checked to see if all needed equipment is available and in good working condition?

_____ Have you made all necessary travel arrangements?

Before the Program

_____ Have you checked out the program area or trail/tour route?

_____ Did you set up all equipment—is it ready to go?

_____ Did you consider appointing and instructing someone to help you with the lights, projector, etc?

Presentation

_____ Any necessary announcements?

_____ Do you have your introduction planned?

_____ Any safety messages (for guided hikes) or other special instructions to visitors?

_____ Do you have your handouts or teaching aids ready?

_____ Do you have your summary or conclusion ready?

Remember that the check list is a tool to make life easier for you. Give it a try for your next program if you're not already using one.

So What

This is the part of the plan where you ask yourself "how will I know if the program accomplished its objectives?" If you refer back to Table 1 in Chapter Three, there is a matrix of evaluation techniques you can use to help you find out how you did. Here is a self-evaluation check list (Lewis, 1983) that might also be of use. (Figures 49a and 49b).

Interpretive Program and Services Plan Check List

Figure 50 is a little one-page planning sheet that I developed some time ago to help volunteer interpretors with program planning. Feel free to copy and use this form.

Self Evaluation

As an interpretor, you will be evaluated by the site or area manager from time to time. Responding to the following statements may help you determine how well you are doing as an interpretor. Check the appropriate block for each statement. You may want to ask others to give points of view. (Lewis, 1983)

ALWAYS ◄─► NEVER

GENERAL ATTITUDE

1. I have an insatiable curiosity.

2. I realize that the search for knowledge is continuous.

3. I have a love for all life.

4. I have a high regard for the incredibly complex ecology that gives special vitality to my park.

5. I have an appreciation for human history of my area.

6. I have a high regard for park visitors.

7. I am concerned for the welfare and safety of visitors.

8. I want visitors to be better informed, inspired and stimulated because of who I am.

9. I want to share myself and what I know with visitors.

10. I treat all visitors equally regardless of age, sex, race; or the way they treat me.

11. I'm cheerful, patient and courteous.

12. I care about my appearance and dress appropriately for my job.

13. I don't put people down for asking "dumb" questions.

14. I start and end all my activities on time.

15. I reach out to people; make myself approachable, available.

16. I believe in what I'm doing.

17. I feel enthusiastic about my work.

18. I try to lighten my approach and use humor when it's appropriate.

19. I'm self-confident without being conceited.

20. I exert a quiet, gentle, but firm leadership.

21. I can walk on water.

UNDERSTANDING OF AUDIENCES

22. I'm aware of some of the reasons people come to my park area.

23. I understand the processes by which people learn.

GOALS OF INTERPRETATION

24. I understand the goals of interpretation.

25. I'm striving to accomplish the goals of interpretation.

PRIMARY ELEMENTS OF INTERPRETATION INVOLVEMENT

26. I arrive early at my activity so I can become acquainted with my group.

27. Before conducting an activity, I have always established a rapport.

28. I'm aware that what I do first is especially important, and give it my special attention.

29. I adapt every presentation to those in the group.

30. I use questioning effectively as an involvement technique.

31. I encourage visitors to use all their senses.

32. I use a variety of structural patterns to make my presentations more involving.

ORGANIZATION

33. Every activity I conduct has a theme.

34. I select main headings which support my theme.

35. I arrange my main headings in an orderly fashion.

36. Introductions to my presentations create a favorable atmosphere and arouse interest in my subject.

37. The conclusions to my presentations inspire my audiences.

GIVING LIFE TO POTENTIALLY DULL SUBJECT

38. I use a variety of support material that's carefully researched.

39. I tell stories, relate anecdotes, employ narration and use visuals in my presentations.

Figure 49a.

40. I'm careful to provide transitions as I move from one idea to another. ☐☐☐☐

41. I select understandable words. ☐☐☐☐

42. Informal, concrete language typifies my presentations. ☐☐☐☐

43. My delivery is enthusiastic, self-assured and physically direct. ☐☐☐☐

44. My style of delivery is friendly, pleasant, informal and casual. ☐☐☐☐

45. I adapt my pace to the situation. ☐☐☐☐

GIVING INFORMATION AND ORIENTATION

46. I try to assess the needs of visitors and give them the amount of information ☐☐☐☐ I think they want.

47. I'm convinced it's important to give accurate information. ☐☐☐☐

48. If I don't know the answer to a visitors' question, I look it up. ☐☐☐☐

49. I reach out to visitors by greeting them. ☐☐☐☐

VISITOR CENTERS

50. I give equal attention to all visitors. ☐☐☐☐

51. I don't make fun of visitors' questions. ☐☐☐☐

52. I listen to understand when I'm hearing complaints. ☐☐☐☐

53. I answer questions as if it's the first time I've been asked them. ☐☐☐☐

54. I use sketches and visuals to enhance the spoken word. ☐☐☐☐

55. I sometimes ask a visitor to paraphrase the directions I've given. ☐☐☐☐

56. I know how to read maps upside-down. ☐☐☐☐

57. I give *interpreted* facts. ☐☐☐☐

58. I'm conscious of the need to provide for the visitors' safety. ☐☐☐☐

ROVING INTERPRETATION

59. I interpret facts only when its appropriate. ☐☐☐☐

60. I sometimes gather groups for mini-walks or mini-tours. ☐☐☐☐

TALKS

61. I mix with the audience during the pre-talk period. ☐☐☐☐

62. I make myself available to visitors for questions after a talk. ☐☐☐☐

63. When I use slides in a talk, I use them as support materials, not as ☐☐☐☐ crutches.

64. I refer to the slides directly only when there is a special reason. ☐☐☐☐

65. The only slides I use are those which support my theme. ☐☐☐☐

66. I don't use slides as cues. ☐☐☐☐

67. I become acquainted with my audience before the program begins. ☐☐☐☐

68. My campfire program doesn't run over 35 minutes. ☐☐☐☐

69. I use recorded music during the pre-talk period only. ☐☐☐☐

70. If I use community singing, I don't overdo it. ☐☐☐☐

71. I use interviews and question-answer periods before the talk when appropriate. ☐☐☐☐

72. I keep my announcements brief. ☐☐☐☐

DEMONSTRATIONS

73. I make sure that what I'm showing is visible. ☐☐☐☐

74. I gather the audience around me for an intimate, easily seen and heard ☐☐☐☐ presentation.

75. My historical demonstrations are accurate, interesting and relevant. ☐☐☐☐

WALKS, TOURS AND HIKES

76. I arrive at the assembly point at least 15 minutes before the activity is ☐☐☐☐ scheduled to begin.

77. I start on time. ☐☐☐☐

78. I warn people of dangers along the way. ☐☐☐☐

79. I explain the reasons for any special restrictions. ☐☐☐☐

80. I move the group in a way which indicates this activity isn't going to be static. ☐☐☐☐

81. I shorten the amount of material I cover when the group is larger. ☐☐☐☐

82. I maintain a pace that's neither tiring nor boring. ☐☐☐☐

83. I have a definite conclusion to my activity. ☐☐☐☐

84. I make sure all can see and hear. ☐☐☐☐

85. I avoid giving a canned spiel. ☐☐☐☐

Figure 49b.

INTERPRETIVE PROGRAM / SERVICE PLAN
CHECK LIST

Program_____

Why? Objectives of the Program or Service.

_____

_____

What? The resource(s) you will be Interpreting:

_____

_____

_____

Who? Who is your intended audience?

Age group_____

Reason they would want to attend the program_____

_____

_____

How/When/Where you will conduct the program:

HOW: Live Demonstration_____ Slide Talk _____ Guest Speaker_____

Interpretive Hike/Walk_____ Other_____

DATE:_____ Time:_____ Program Location:_____

So What - How will you know if your program objectives are met?

_____

_____

_____

Implementation / Operation - What do you need to present the program?

_____

_____

_____

(Use the back of this sheet if necessary)

Figure 50.

Planning Your Presentation

As you plan your interpretive program there are a number of factors involved in presenting an intriguing, emotional, and successfully conducted activity. The following check list is useful in helping to plan and present your program.

Introduction

_____ Create a favorable atmosphere with your audience. Arrive early to meet them informally, introduce yourself, learn a few of their names (relate).

_____ Arouse interest in your subject and program (provoke).

_____ Clarify the purpose of your program or presentation.

Creating a Favorable Atmosphere

_____ Refer to current interests of the audience (relate).

_____ Respond to the mood of the audience.

_____ Refer to special interests of the audience (relate).

_____ Compliment the audience.

Arousing Interest In Your Subject

_____ Ask one or more stimulating questions (provoke).

_____ Use an unusual statement (Did you know that...?).

_____ Relate a relevant personal story to the audience.

_____ Use a provocative quotation.

_____ Refer to a problem (pollution, vandalism, etc.).

_____ Use an illustration or other visual aid.

Conclusion

_____ Summarize your main points and theme.

_____ Raise questions as to what's next.

_____ Use an inspirational tone and challenge the audience.

_____ Script a strong, memorable final sentence.

Delivery is the physical process by which a message is conveyed. It includes such elements as the way a person walks, stands, sits, gestures, uses his or her voice, etc. There are a few general principles of delivery that should be useful to consider as you plan your program presentation.

- Be enthusiastic.
- Feel self assured.
- Use a variety of techniques.
- Be physically direct.
- Use abundant body gestures (non-verbals).
- Be friendly, pleasant, informal, and casual.
- Adapt your pace to the situation.

Preparing for the Presentation—Tips to Remember

1. Know what you are going to try to put across; don't ramble.
2. Your audience is going to be diverse, with all sorts of preconceptions about their upcoming experience. Bring all of their minds together at the beginning of the program by emphasizing one or two concepts around which your talk will revolve. This unites the group and gets everyone off to a good start.
3. Organize your data in a logical sequence around your major theme. Make it easy for the audience to absorb and remember the main points.
4. Be sure of your facts. Remember that the audience doesn't hear "I *think* it's a...." from your talk. You are the authority.
5. Outline the main points of your presentation. Focus on no more than five major points.
6. Don't grind on with facts. Remember you are "illustrating" a theme.
7. The story is the thing. A good interpretive program is a well-developed and crafted story that is illustrated with objects, photos, artifacts, or other visual or sensory aides.
8. Keep the presentation short—45 minutes or so.
9. Use humor, jokes, etc. in your presentation. Remember, your audience is often on vacation. They want to have a good time.

Structuring

Structuring is providing the visitors with guidance. It can give the visitors an idea of what the program may consist of, let them know what is expected of them, ease insecurities about the program, direct movements, and suggest activities. Structuring is most effective when it is planned and reveals to the visitor the steps to your objectives.

Introductions

Your introduction at the beginning of a program establishes the climate you expect to maintain throughout. It's your opportunity to let the visitors know you will take care of their needs as well as provide an enlightening and enjoyable experience. Certain points should be included in the introduction:

- Who you are.
- What is going to happen.
- Where you're going.
- Where you'll end up.
- How long it is going to take.
- What will be required of the visitors.
- What's the objective of the program or tour.

These details allow the visitors to decide immediately if the program will meet their safety and security needs. When these needs are met, the visitors will be more receptive to your program.

Transitions

Further structuring can take place by letting the visitor know what they might do as they move to the next portion of an activity. For example, "What I'd like you to do is to follow me down this trail and as we are walking, look for evidence that humans have been here before. When we get to the bottom of the trail, I'll ask you to share your observations and tell what you saw that indicated human's presence here."

Be Creative

Discovery consists of looking at the same thing as everyone else and thinking something different.

Remember to be Interpretive!

With all of this program planning, remember that for the program to be *interpretive* it must employ interpretive techniques and principles. As you are planning the content (story) and the ways you will be illustrating the theme, remember that the presentation must:

- **Provoke** curiosity and interest.
- **Relate** to the everyday life of the visitors.
- **Reveal** the main points through a different or unique viewpoint.
- Address the whole (**theme**).
- Have **message unity**.

You may want to refer back to Chapter Two for examples of how to use all of these principles in developing your interpretive presentation.

References

Gross, M. and R. Zimmerman. 1990. *The Interpreter's Guidebook: Techniques for Programs and Presentations.* College of Natural Resources, University of Wisconsin-Stevens Point.

Ham, S.H. 1992. *Environmental Interpretation: A Practical Guide for People with Big Ideas and Small Budgets.* Golden, CO: North American Press.

Lewis, W.J. 1988. *Interpreting for Park Visitors.* Philadelphia, PA: Eastern National Park and Monument Association.

Tilden, F. 1957. *Interpreting our Heritage.* The University of North Carolina Press, Chapel Hill.

Veverka, J.A. 1988. *U.S. Army Corps of Engineers Interpretive Services Manual.* U.S. Government Printing Office.

Index